TAYLOR

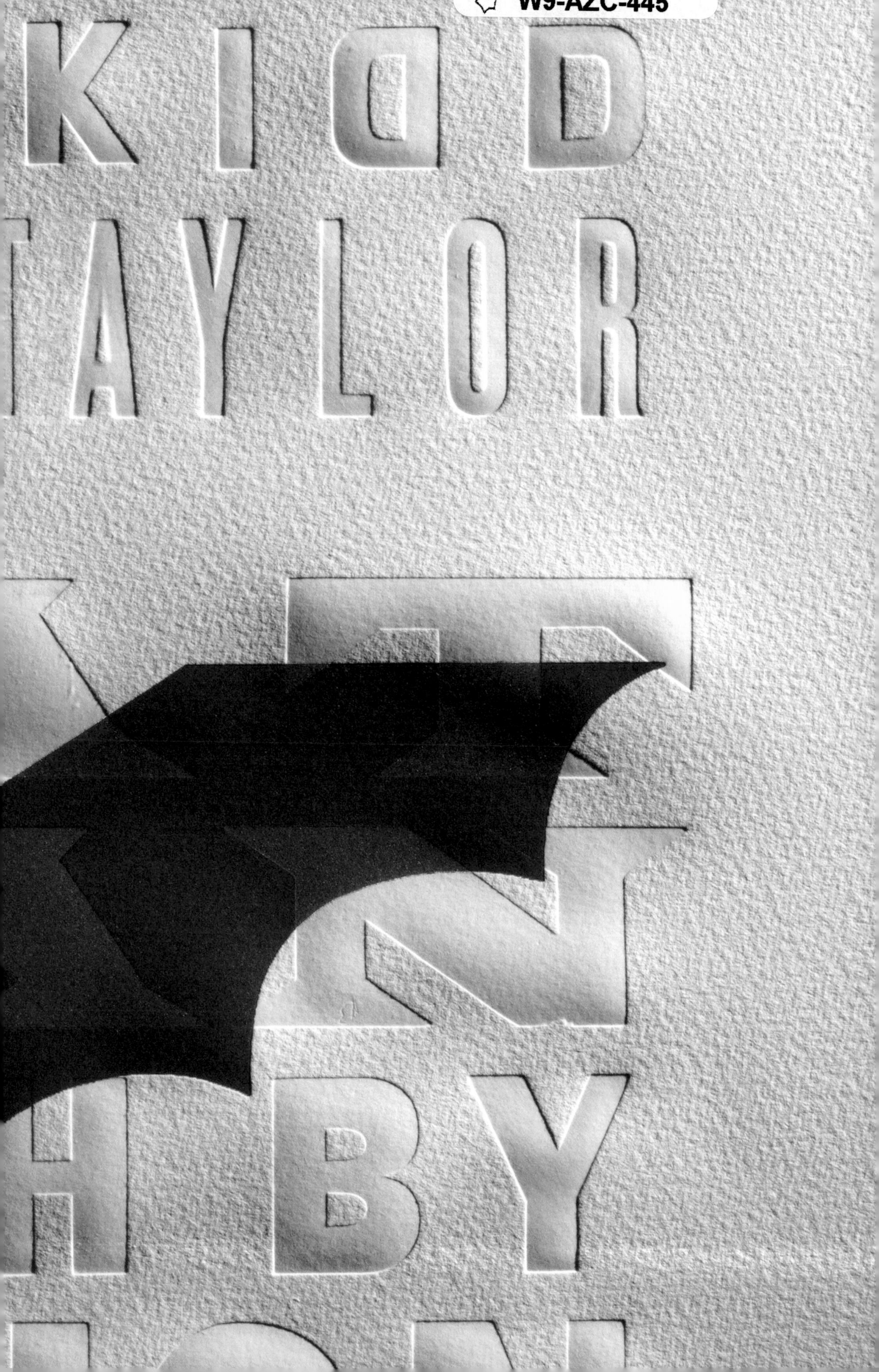

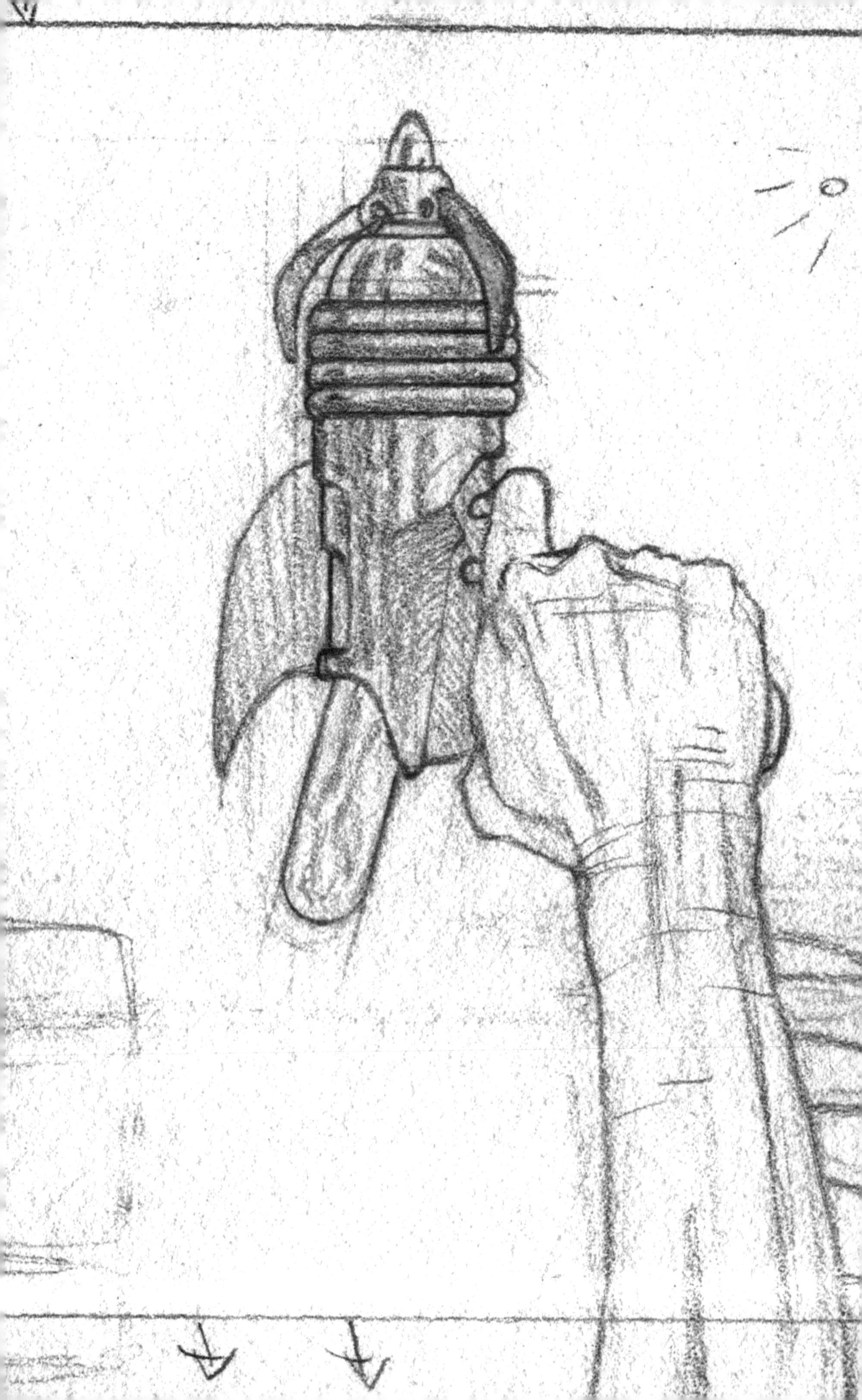

BATMAN
DEATH BY DESIGN
CHIP KIDD · DAVE TAYLOR

BATMAN
DEATH BY DESIGN
CHIP KIDD

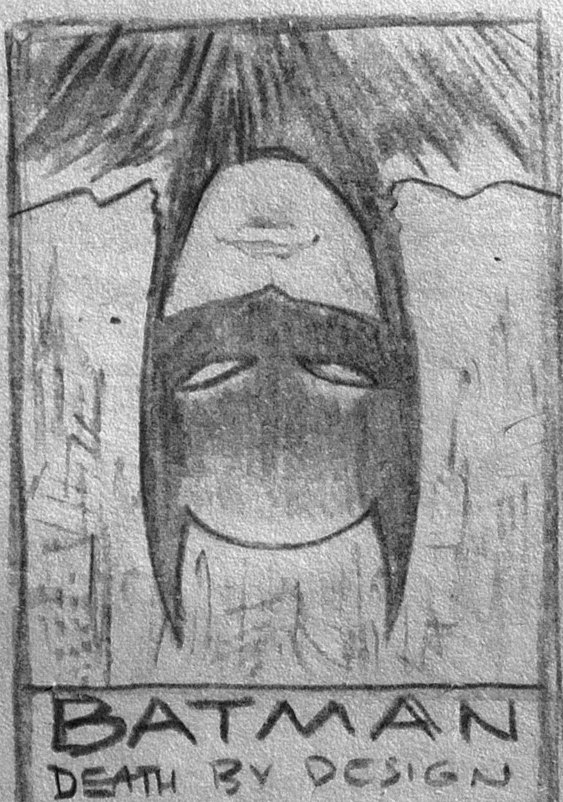
BATMAN
DEATH BY DESIGN
CHIP KIDD · DAVE TAYLOR

BATMAN
DEATH BY DESIGN
CHIP KIDD
BATMAN

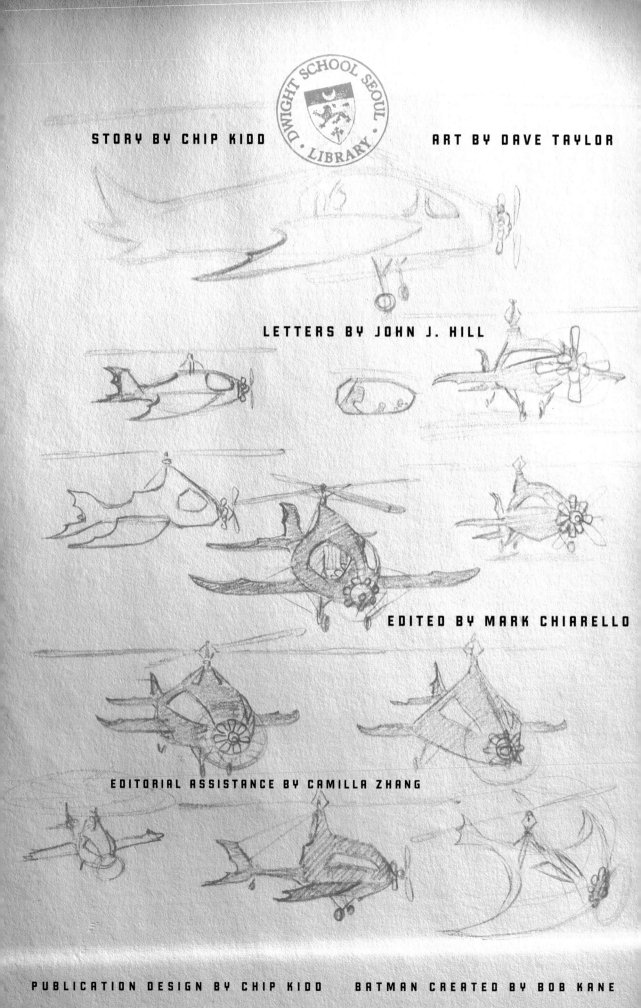

STORY BY CHIP KIDD

ART BY DAVE TAYLOR

LETTERS BY JOHN J. HILL

EDITED BY MARK CHIARELLO

EDITORIAL ASSISTANCE BY CAMILLA ZHANG

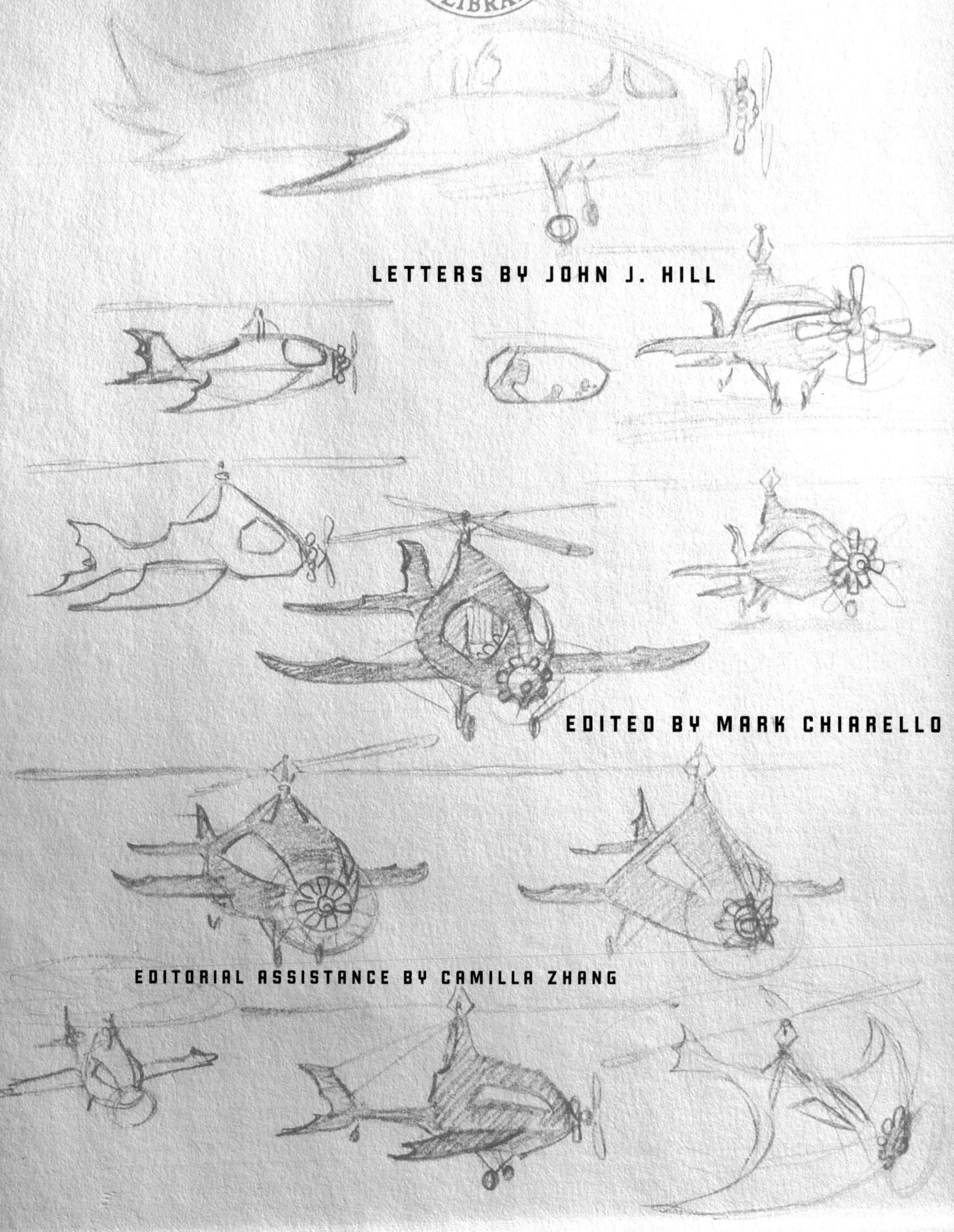

PUBLICATION DESIGN BY CHIP KIDD

BATMAN CREATED BY BOB KANE

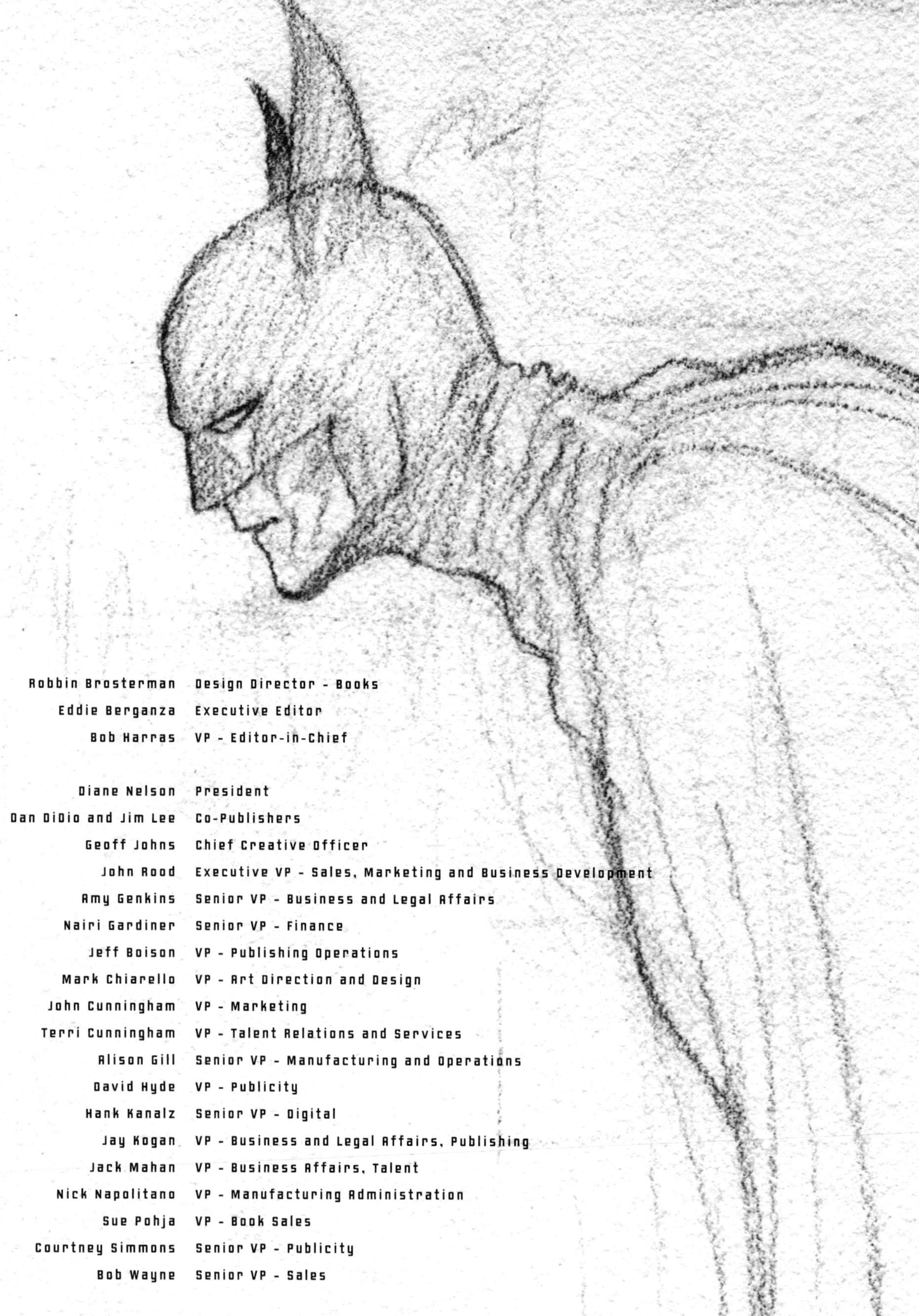

BATMAN: Death by Design

DC Comics, 1700 Broadway, New York, NY 10019. A Warner Bros. Entertainment Company. Printed by RR Donnelley, Salem, VA, USA. 5/2/12. First Printing. ISBN:978-1-4012-3453-9

Library of Congress Cataloging-in-Publication Data

Kidd, Chip.
Batman : death by design / Chip Kidd, Dave Taylor.
p. cm.
ISBN 978-1-4012-3453-9
1. Graphic novels. I. Taylor, Dave. II. Title.
PN6728.B36K54 2012
741.5'973--dc23

2011051791

SUSTAINABLE FORESTRY INITIATIVE
Certified Chain of Custody
At Least 25% Certified Forest Content
www.sfiprogram.org
SFI-01042
APPLIES TO TEXT STOCK ONLY

ACKNOWLEDGMENTS.

Dave Taylor exceeded my expectations for the art in this book. And my expectations were higher than the Wayne Central Station (see below). This project would not have been possible without Neil Gaiman and Dan DiDio. Mark Chiarello improved it immensely, and Camilla Zhang and Louis Prandi provided invaluable assistance. — C. K.

This book is dedicated to Andrew Loomis and Hugh Ferriss whose work drove this project from the beginning. — D. T.

For Sandy, Bart, Peggy, and Inger. —C. K.

For my wife and daughter, without whom this book would not exist, my Mom for her dogged determination, and for my Father who taught me how to sharpen a pencil correctly.. —D. T.

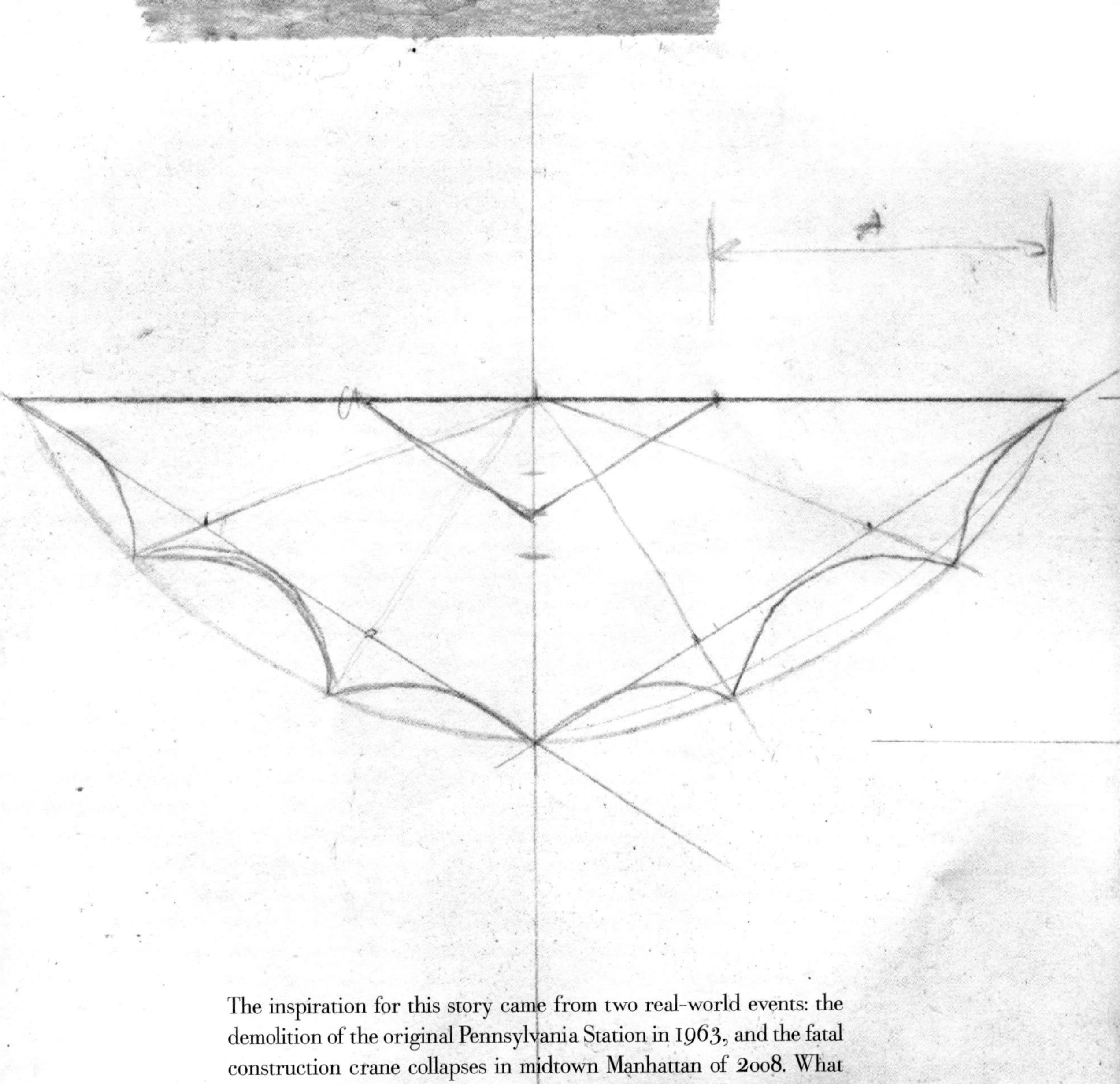

The inspiration for this story came from two real-world events: the demolition of the original Pennsylvania Station in 1963, and the fatal construction crane collapses in midtown Manhattan of 2008. What if, despite the years, they were somehow connected? And what if they happened in Gotham City, during a glorious, golden age . . .

OKAY, HERE WE GO. BETA-TESTING GRAPPLE-TRON PROTOTYPE VERSION THREE. THE FIRST TWO WERE SPRING-LOADED, LIMITED RANGE. THIS ONE'S POWERED BY A MICRO-IONIZED REACTOR. ALFRED'S IDEA.

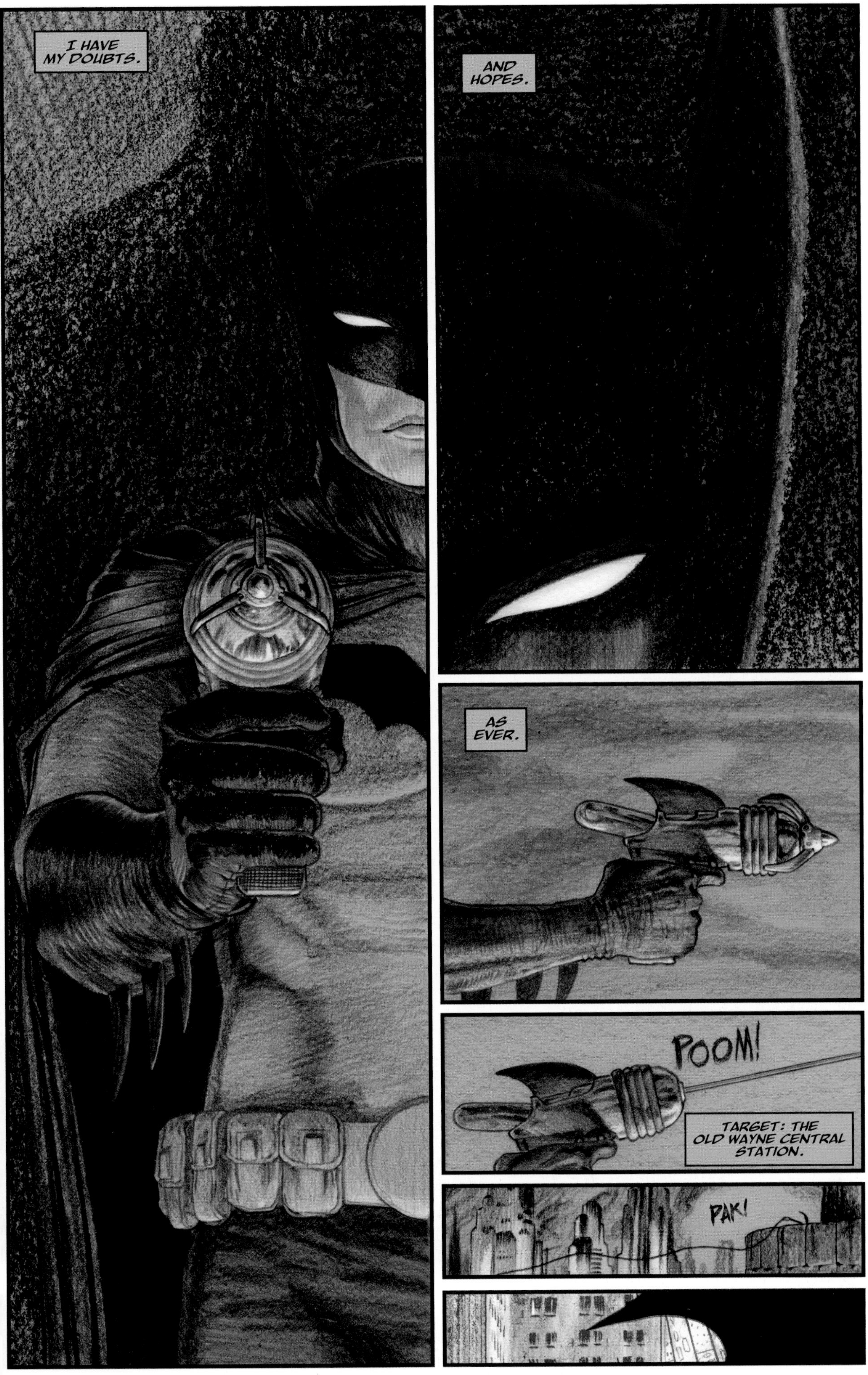

I HAVE MY DOUBTS.

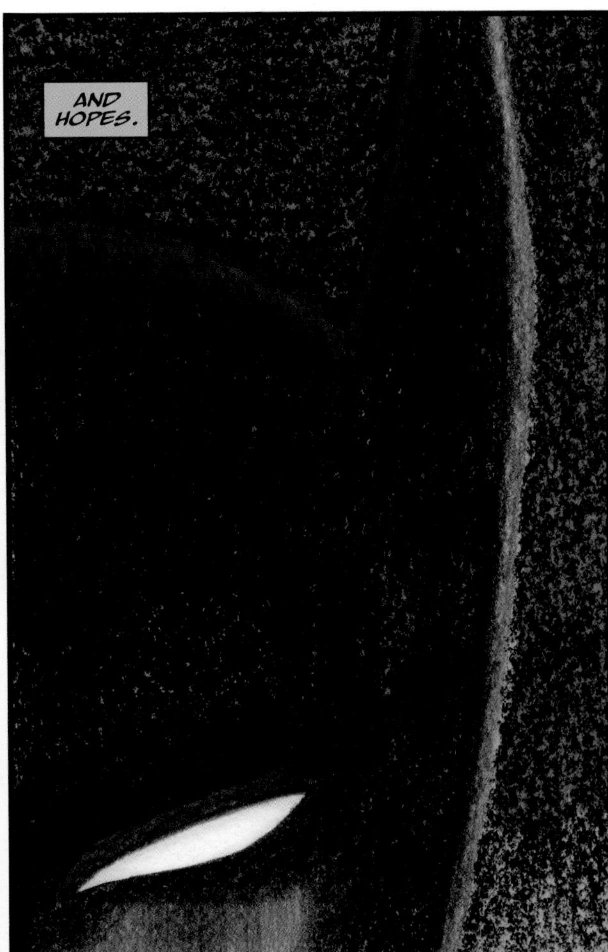

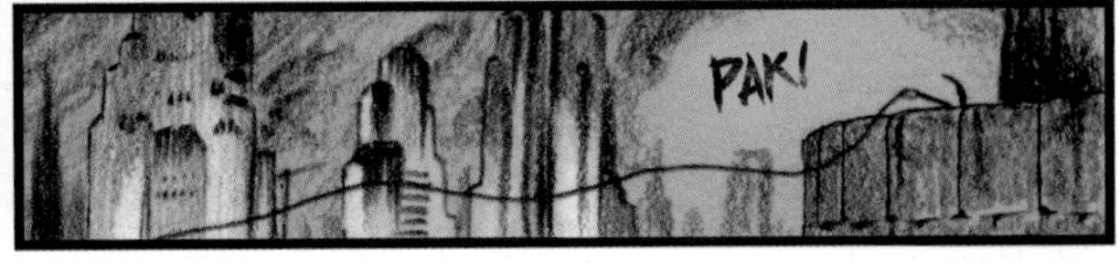

WILL I
MISS IT?
KIDD

TAYLOR

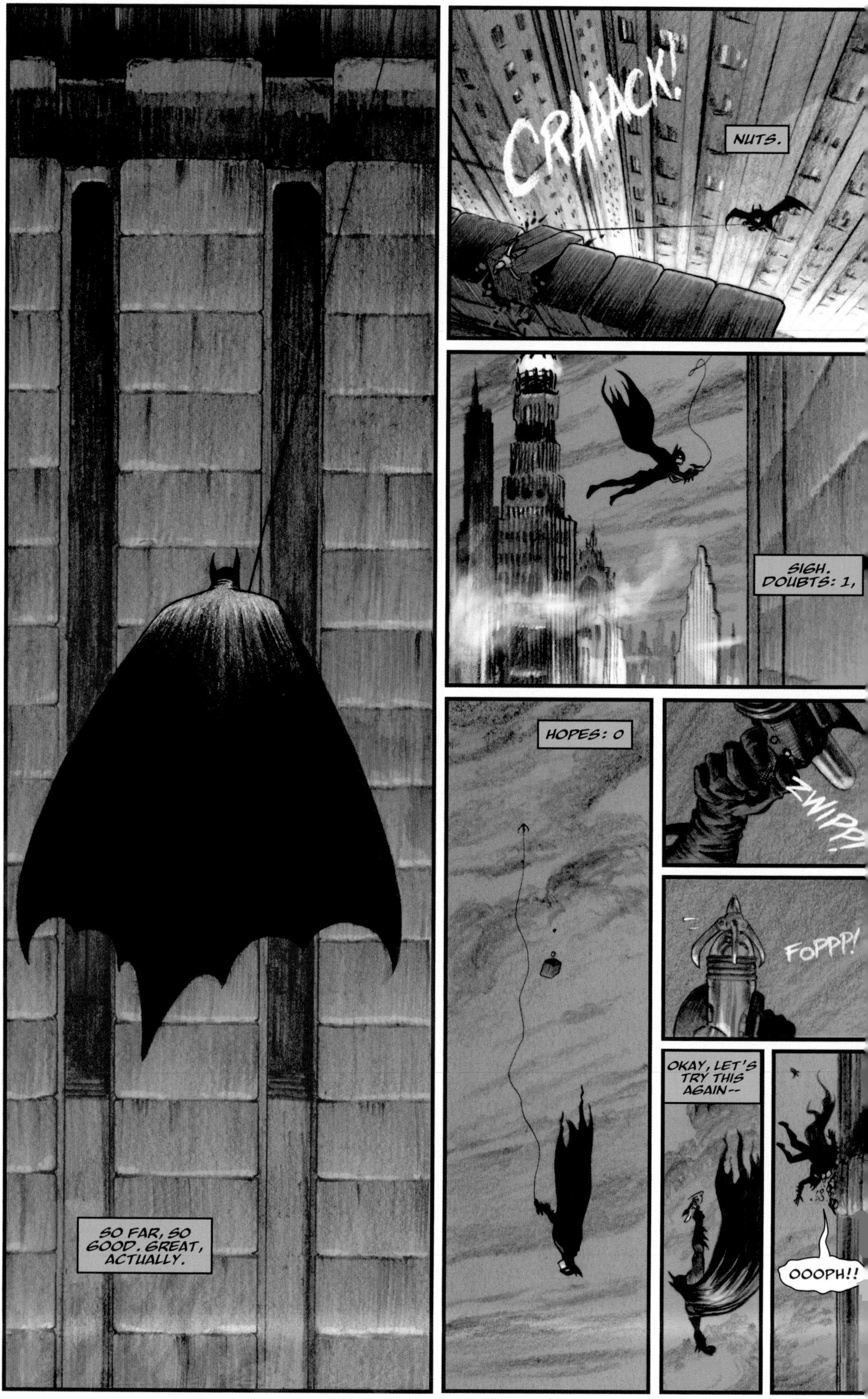

SO FAR, SO GOOD. GREAT, ACTUALLY.

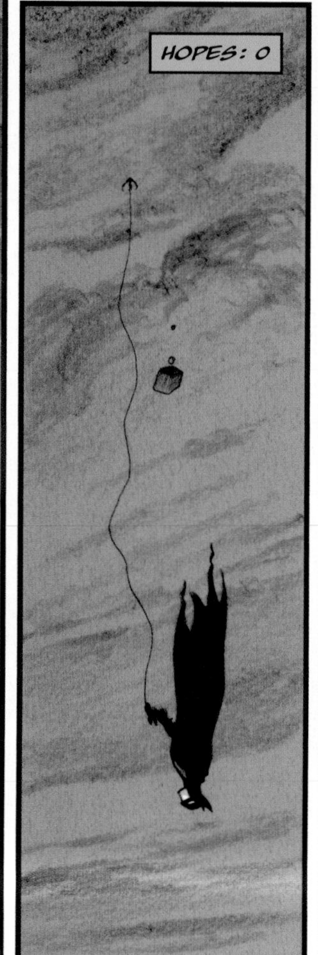

ZWIPP!

FOPPP!

OKAY, LET'S TRY THIS AGAIN--

OOOPH!!

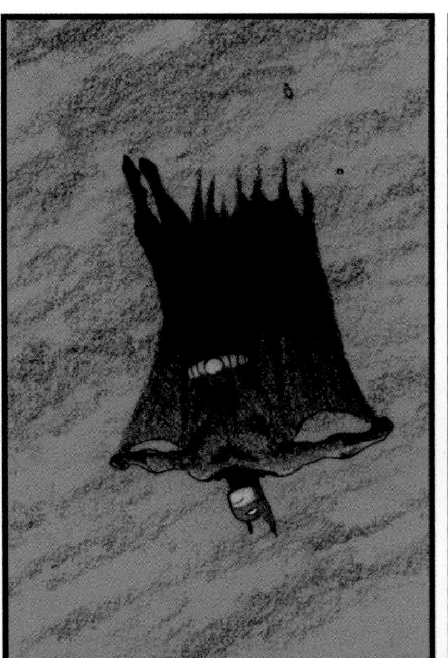

THAT WAS SMOOTH.

NO, YOU OLD LUMP. I WON'T MISS YOU AT ALL.

CITIZENS OF GOTHAM. I STAND BEFORE YOU, HUMBLED AT THE PROSPECT OF THIS OPPORTUNITY. THE OLD WAYNE CENTRAL STATION HAS LONG SINCE SERVED ITS PURPOSE. AND SO WE BID IT FAREWELL. DECADES AGO, BEFORE I WAS BORN, MY FATHER COMMISSIONED IT WITH THE HOPE THAT IT WOULD LITERALLY BRING THE PEOPLE OF THIS CITY TOGETHER.

AND FOR A LONG TIME, IT DID. BUT THE CITY HAS CHANGED. AND WITH IT, THE HABITS AND THE NEEDS OF ITS PEOPLE, AND THE OLD STATION HAS LONG SINCE BECOME UNUSED AND OBSOLETE.

WHICH MEANS IT'S TIME TO MAKE WAY FOR THE FUTURE. IT'S THE DAWN OF A NEW AGE FOR GOTHAM, NOT JUST RIGHT HERE, BUT ALL ACROSS THE CITY. WE ARE GROWING, BUILDING, PROGRESSING, ON OUR WAY TO A BRIGHTER FUTURE. AND ***THIS*** WILL BE OUR GATEWAY: TODAY WE BREAK GROUND ON THE ***NEW*** WAYNE CENTRAL STA--

SHRAAAAAAANNNNKHHHH

BATMAN: DEA

TH BY DESIGN

MASSIVE CRANE COLLAPSE IN MIDTOWN

Cause Still Undetermined.

By Richard Frank

GOTHAM GAZETTE. NEWSROOM.

≠BZZZT≠ FRANK, IN HERE PLEASE.

RICHARD FRANK. NEWLY HIRED ARCHITECTURAL CRITIC FOR THE PAPER. JUST OUT OF HARVARD.
OH, GREAT.
YES CHIEF.

THE GAZETTE IS TAKING A BIG CHANCE ON HIM. HE KNOWS IT.
WHAT'S UP?

ELLIOT OSBOURNE. EDITOR-IN-CHIEF OF THE GAZETTE, FOR AS LONG AS ANYONE CAN REMEMBER. TWO PULITZERS. SEEN IT ALL AND CORRECTED THE SPELLING. CUT HIM, HE BLEEDS INK.
NICE JOB ON THE CRANE STORY. I WANT TO KEEP YOU ON IT. SEE IT THROUGH.

WHAT? I'M NOT AN INVESTIGATIVE REPORTER. I WAS JUST THERE AT THE SCENE.
BUT SIR, I--

Doc Arkham 770. 492
FIND
Bruce Wayne 271 939
SAVE IT. YOU WERE AT THE SCENE. CLOSE THE DOOR.

SIR, I WAS AT THE SCENE AS A *CRITIC.* THIS WHOLE THING, IT'S A COINCIDENCE.

KID, I AM HEREBY DECLARING: ON THIS STORY, YOU ARE NOW A *REPORTER.* ***THE*** REPORTER.
CONSTRUCTION CRANES SIMPLY DO NOT JUST PLUMMET FROM THE HEAVENS.
NARROWLY MISSING ONE OF THE CITY'S MOST PROMINENT CITIZENS.
ON THE OCCASION OF HIS FINALLY CONFIRMING THE EXTREMELY CONTROVERSIAL DEMOLITION OF WHAT MANY HAVE CALLED A MAJOR MONUMENT TO HIS BELOVED FATHER'S LEGACY.
YOUR BEING THERE TO WAX WITTILY ON THE CEREMONY NOTWITHSTANDING, COINCIDENCE THIS IS NOT. NOT IN THIS TOWN.
YOU WILL PURSUE THIS.

YESSIR.

GOD. WHERE...

WHERE DO I START?
...THIS IS WGKO, GOTHAM. STILL NO WORD ON THE CAUSE OF MONDAY'S CATASTROPHIC CRANE COLLAPSE IN MIDTOWN, WHICH LEFT SCORES OF INJURED BUT NO REPORTED FATALITIES. THEY'RE CALLING IT A MIRACLE THAT PHILANTHROPIST BRUCE WAYNE, GIVING A SPEECH ACROSS THE STREET AT THE TIME, IN THE DIRECT PATH OF THE PLUMMETING MACHINE, ESCAPED WITH WHAT HE CALLED ONLY A FEW MINOR SCRAPES.
WHEN ASKED HOW THIS WILL AFFECT THE DEMOLITION AND REBUILDING OF THE ADJACENT WAYNE CENTRAL STATION, MR. WAYNE HAD NO COMMENT. BUT AUTHORITIES REPORTED THAT FOR NOW THE PROJECT IS ON HOLD, WHILE THE CONSIDERABLE JOB OF CLEANING UP THE AFTERMATH OF THE ACCIDENT WILL TAKE WEEKS, IF NOT MONTHS. INSPECTORS HAVE--
BRRRRZT
...IN A RELATED STORY, BART LOAR, UNION PRESIDENT OF CONSTRUCTION LOCAL 27, SAYS THAT THE CRANE COLLAPSE IS YET ANOTHER EXAMPLE OF MANAGERIAL OVERSIGHT, PUTTING HIS WORKERS IN AN UNACCEPTABLY DANGEROUS WORKPLACE.
LOAR, WHEN ASKED IF THE CAUSE COULD HAVE POSSIBLY BEEN DUE TO FAULT OPERATION BY A UNION MEMBER, MADE A SUGGESTION TO THIS REPORTER THAT WOULD HAVE BEEN PHYSICALLY IMPOSSIBLE. THIS IS WXRT, GOTH--
BZZOO

...MOVIE-TONE NEWS. INTERNATIONALLY ACCLAIMED ARCHITECT KEM ROOMHAUS, WHO'S SET TO MAKE HIS GOTHAM DEBUT NEXT WEEK WITH THE SPECTACULAR CEILING NIGHT CLUB, UNVEILS A MODEL OF HIS WINNING DESIGN FOR THE NEW WAYNE CENTRAL STATION BUILDING, WHICH HE CALLS "THE FUTURE OF ARCHITECTURE."
THE NATIVE OF HOLLAND CLAIMS THAT HE IS OFTEN FRIGHTENED OF HIS OWN GENIUS; WHILE SEVERAL NOTABLE CRITICS HAVE CLAIMED THAT THERE'S ACTUALLY NOTHING TO BE SCARED OF. MOVING ON, WE--
ZZZRRRP
...WGOG, WEST GOTHAM. THE MYSTERIOUS DISAPPEARANCE OF GREGOR GREENSIDE CONTINUES TO BAFFLE AUTHORITIES. THE ONCE-VENERATED ARCHITECT WAS REPORTED MISSING ON MONDAY BY HIS SON GARNETT, WHEN HE FAILED TO SHOW UP AT THE OFFICE THEY SHARE IN THE MARSHALL DISTRICT.
GREENSIDE, PRACTICALLY A HOUSEHOLD NAME AT THE HEIGHT OF HIS FAME, HAD LONG SINCE FALLEN INTO OBSCURITY. 87% OF GOTHAMITES POLLED ON THE STREET YESTERDAY BY THE GOTHAM GAZETTE RESPONDED THAT THEY THOUGHT HE HAD DIED AT LEAST TEN YEARS AGO. NEXT UP--
SZZRRRMMM
. . . AN OPPORTUNITY BORN FROM TRAGEDY. THAT'S WHAT SELF-PROCLAIMED "URBAN PRESERVATIONIST" CYNDIA SYL CALLED MONDAY'S CRANE COLLAPSE, WHICH HAS FOR NOW HALTED PLANS TO DEMOLISH THE DERELICT WAYNE CENTRAL STATION.
SYL, A SOCIETY FIXTURE WHO HAS TAKEN UP THE CAUSE OF WHAT SHE SEES AS AN ARCHITECTURAL MASTERPIECE THAT'S BEEN NEARLY DESTROYED BY NEGLECT, MAINTAINS THAT IT'S NOT TOO LATE TO SAVE IT. WE GO NOW TO--
SPRRRRPPP
OH, GOD. CYNDIA SYL...

...I NEARLY FORGOT.
MR. WAYNE, YOUR TEN O'CLOCK IS HERE. MISS SYL.

OKAY, LET'S GET THIS OVER WITH.
OKAY, LET'S GET THIS OVER WITH. THANKS, LORIEL. SEND HER IN, PLEASE.

UM... I ALREADY DID.

YIKES.

AHEM.

I'M-- I'M SORRY. WELCOME, MISS--.
CYNDIA, PLEASE.

I DON'T CARE HOW BEAUTIFUL SHE IS. I'M SHUTTING THIS DOWN AS SOON AS I KNOW WHAT I NEED TO.
CYNDIA. HAVE A SEAT. AND IT'S BRUCE.

THANK YOU, MR., I MEAN...WELL, I'LL JUST COME OUT WITH IT. I WOULD IMAGINE YOU KNOW WHY I'M HERE.

I HAVE AN IDEA, YES.

WELL, I'LL JUST LAY IT ON THE TABLE THEN...

MR. WAYNE, YOU'RE IN A VERY UNIQUE POSITION TO DEFEND THIS CITY.

I'M... AWARE OF THAT.

THEN DEFEND IT. PLEASE. I DON'T KNOW HOW ELSE TO SAY IT. THE WAYNE CENTRAL STATION IS--

A CRUMBLING HULK. THAT'S--

THAT'S ALSO THE SINGLE BEST EXAMPLE OF PATRI-MONUMENTAL MODERNISM IN AMERICA. IT'S ONE OF THE CITY'S-- THE COUNTRY'S!--GREATEST TREASURES OF URBAN ARCHITECTURE. OF COURSE IT'S CRUMBLING, NO ONE'S LOOKED AFTER IT FOR CLOSE TO TWENTY YEARS.

WHEN YOUR FATHER COMMISSIONED GREGOR GREENSIDE TO DESIGN AND BUILD THE STATION, HIS INSTRUCTIONS WERE: "REMEMBER, FOR ANYONE COMING TO GOTHAM, WHEN THEY DEPART THE TRAIN, THIS WILL BE THE FIRST THING THEY SEE OF THE CITY.

"I WANT THEM TO KNOW THEY'VE COME TO THE MOST REMARKABLE PLACE ON EARTH. YOU MUST ASTONISH THEM." AND THAT'S EXACTLY WHAT HE DID--IT INSTANTLY BECAME AN INTERNATIONAL DESTINATION FOR TOURISTS AND ARCHITECTURAL HISTORIANS ALIKE. GREGOR FULFILLED YOUR FATHER'S MANDATE.

YES, AND THAT WAS THE PROBLEM. GREENSIDE'S MANTRA HAS BEEN WELL DOCUMENTED: "EFFECT BEFORE EVERYTHING." AND THAT INCLUDED STRUCTURAL INTEGRITY. THE SOARING VAULT OF THE RECEPTION AREA WASN'T BOLSTERED WITH STRUTS THAT WOULD HAVE INTERRUPTED THE SPACE WHILE PROVIDING THE NECESSARY SUPPORT.

INSTEAD, THE OUTER SKIN WAS SUPPOSED TO DO THAT. AND IT COULD HAVE, HAD IT BEEN PROPERLY FORTIFIED. BUT IT WASN'T, AND WITH TIME, IT STARTED TO DECOMPOSE. THEN, ALTERNATIVE MASS TRANSIT CHOICES STARTED POPPING UP. AND THE EXPLOSION OF AUTOMOBILES. IT WAS CLEAR WHERE THINGS WERE GOING, LITERALLY.

IN SHORT, MISS SYL, HERE ARE THE FACTS: AT THIS POINT, TO PROPERLY RESTORE WAYNE CENTRAL STATION AS IT EXISTS NOW WOULD ACTUALLY COST MORE THAN SIMPLY TEARING IT DOWN AND STARTING ALL OVER AGAIN. I'M SORRY, BUT THAT'S THE UNDENIABLE TRUTH.

SO, THIS IS JUST ABOUT MONEY? REALLY? FORGIVE MY PRESUMPTION, BUT WHY IS THAT A PROBLEM FOR *YOU*?
LOOK, I *CARE* ABOUT THIS. I'D BE HAPPY TO DEDICATE ALL OF MY TIME TO MAKING THIS HAPPEN. THE HISTORY OF THIS BUILDING WAS MY GRADUATE THESIS. I COULD DO FUND-RAISING, GIVE LECTURES ABOUT THE STRUCTURE, ANYTHING.

THIS IS NOT GOOD. EVERYTHING I'D READ, SEEN, I WAS READY TO HATE HER. I WAS COUNTING ON IT. I'M MUCH, MUCH BETTER WITH PEOPLE I CAN'T *STAND*. SHE SHOULD BE AN OVERPRIVILEGED, SELF-ENTITLED, SPOILED, SANCTIMONIOUS SNOT. LIKE ME.
NOT THIS. NOT SO IMPASSIONED, INFORMED. NOT SO IMPERFECTLY PERFECT.

GOOD GOD. IT'S UNBEARABLE. NOT BECAUSE HE'S SO DAMNED CUTE, ARTICULATE, WELL-MANNERED AND SMART. AND DUH, POWERFUL.
IT'S BECAUSE IN SPITE OF ALL THAT, NO MATTER HOW HE TRIES TO HIDE IT...
...HE'S JUST SO *SAD*.

THIS *SHOULD* BE ABOUT YOUR FATHER'S LEGACY. YOUR LEGACY. TO GOTHAM.

I AM WELL AWARE OF MY LEGACY TO THIS CITY. AND I AM BUILDING IT. MY *OWN* WAY.

SO MUCH FOR SAD. MAKE THAT PISSED OFF.
WELL. I GUESS THAT'S IT THEN. BEFORE I GO, WOULD YOU AT LEAST ANSWER ONE QUESTION?

CERTAINLY.

WHY DID YOU EVEN AGREE TO MEET WITH ME?

YOU HAD EVERYTHING TO GAIN FROM THE CRANE ACCIDENT. AND PROBABLY THE MEANS TO MAKE IT HAPPEN. BUT NOW...
BECAUSE. BECAUSE I --

OH, SKIP IT. I *KNOW* THAT LOOK. WOLF!

CLOSE ENOUGH, I GUESS.
MISS SYL, CYNDIA, PLEASE! --

IS IT COMPLETELY OUT OF THE QUESTION TO CONSIDER THAT THE LADY MIGHT HAVE A POINT, SIR?
ALFRED, I CAN'T EXACTLY TELL HER THAT BUILDING MY OWN COVERT TRANSIT HUB UNDER THE SITE WILL BE MUCH, MUCH EASIER IF WE RAZE THE BUILDING. SOMEHOW I DON'T THINK THAT WILL SWAY HER.

BESIDES, ROOMHAUS MAY BE AN INSUFFERABLE, AFFECTED, NARCISSISTIC CREEP, BUT HE'S ALSO A GENIUS. HE WON THE COMPETITION FOR A REASON.
HIS PLAN TO RECYCLE THE CARBON EMISSIONS FROM IN AND AROUND THE STATION TO NOURISH ALL THE FLORA INSIDE IT IS INSPIRED.

SPEAKING OF MR. ROOMHAUS, SIR. YOU'VE RECEIVED AN INVITATION, TO THE OPENING OF HIS NIGHTCLUB, THE CEILING.

PERHAPS THIS COULD BE AN OPPORTUNITY TO CONVINCE THE LADY OF THE...CREEP'S PROWESS.

HELLO?
CYNDIA, IT'S BRUCE WAYNE. PLEASE DON'T HANG UP.
HMMPF. YOU HAVE 10 SECONDS TO TELL ME WHY I SHOULDN'T.
THE CREAM OF GOTHAM IS HIGH IN THE SKY TONIGHT, AT THE OPENING OF WHAT IS BEING BILLED AS THE WORLD'S MOST GLAMOROUS NIGHTCLUB, THE CEILING. AND WHAT A SIGHT IT IS, WHERE PATRONS CAN FEEL LIKE THEY'RE DINING AND DANCING ON AIR. ARCHITECT KEM ROOMHAUS DESCRIBES IT AS REDUCTIVE DESIGN TAKEN TO ITS ULTIMATE EXTREME, INTRODUCING A BRAND NEW SCHOOL OF ARCHITECTURE HE CALLS MINI-MAXIMALISM.

I WANT TO APOLOGIZE. AND EXPLAIN. YOU HAD THE WRONG IDEA, COMPLETELY.
DOES THIS MEAN YOU'RE RECONSIDERING ON THE STATION?
WELL, NO. BUT, IF YOU'LL ALLOW ME TO TAKE YOU TO DINNER, I CAN SHOW YOU FIRST-HAND THE TALENT BEHIND THE NEW PROPOSAL. PLEASE.
SHOW ME? AT DINNER?

NO!! IT'S MAXI-MINIMALISM!

YOU FOOL.

AND HERE'S BRUCE WAYNE WITH... CYNDIA SYL?! MR. WAYNE! IS THERE ROMANCE IN THE AIR?

OH, I--

DEFINITELY NOT. YOU'RE SMELLING THE STERNO FROM THE BUFFET TABLES. MOVE ALONG, JUNIOR.

SORRY ABOUT THAT.

CHECK YOUR BAG, SIR?

OH, I'LL KEEP IT WITH ME, THANKS.
CHAMPAGNE?
NOT RIGHT NOW, THANKS.
SOMETHING DOESN'T FEEL RIGHT. OR AM I BEING PARANOID?

CHAMPAGNE, MISS?
SURE. WHY NOT?

SO, WHAT DO YOU THINK?
WELL, AS LONG AS I DON'T LOOK...

...DOWN. OH. OH MY GOD.

YEEK!

UM...

...SORRY. ABOUT THAT.

OH, NO TROUBLE.
HOPE I DIDN'T GET ANY STERNO ON YOU.

LET'S SIT.

BEFORE I YAWN IN TECHNI-COLOR.

OKAY, I'LL ADMIT: AS A SITE-SPECIFIC STUNT, IT'S AMAZING. BUT AS A SERIOUS, LASTING WORK OF ARCHITECTURE? NO. COME ON.
HOW CAN YOU MEAN THAT?

NIGHTCLUBS COME AND GO. SO WHAT DOES THIS BECOME WHEN THE CEILING'S PASSÉ? CONDOS? I DON'T THINK SO. IT'S A SLAB OF GLASS.
GOODNESS. YOU CERTAINLY ARE JADED.

WHAT, FOR TAKING THE LONG VIEW? THAT'S NOT JADED, IT'S COMMON SENSE. I... HUH-HAMPF.
WHAT?

GOD, THE WAY I GRABBED YOU LIKE THAT, I'M SORRY, IT'S--HUH-HA, IT'S FUNNY, I HUH-HA!
CYNDIA?
OH, NO.

I GRABBED YOU!! HA HA HA HA HA HA HA! AND WE BARELY KNOW EACH OTHER!! HA HA HA HA HA HA HA HA HA HA HA!!!!!
NO NO NO NO NO--

CYNDIA!!

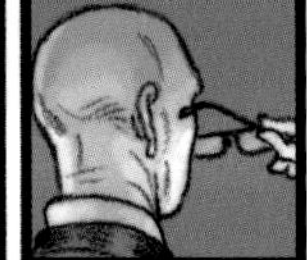

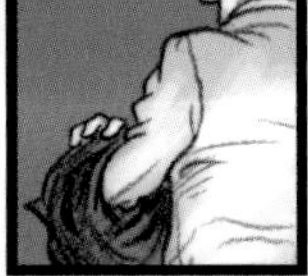

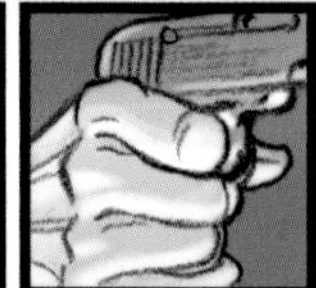

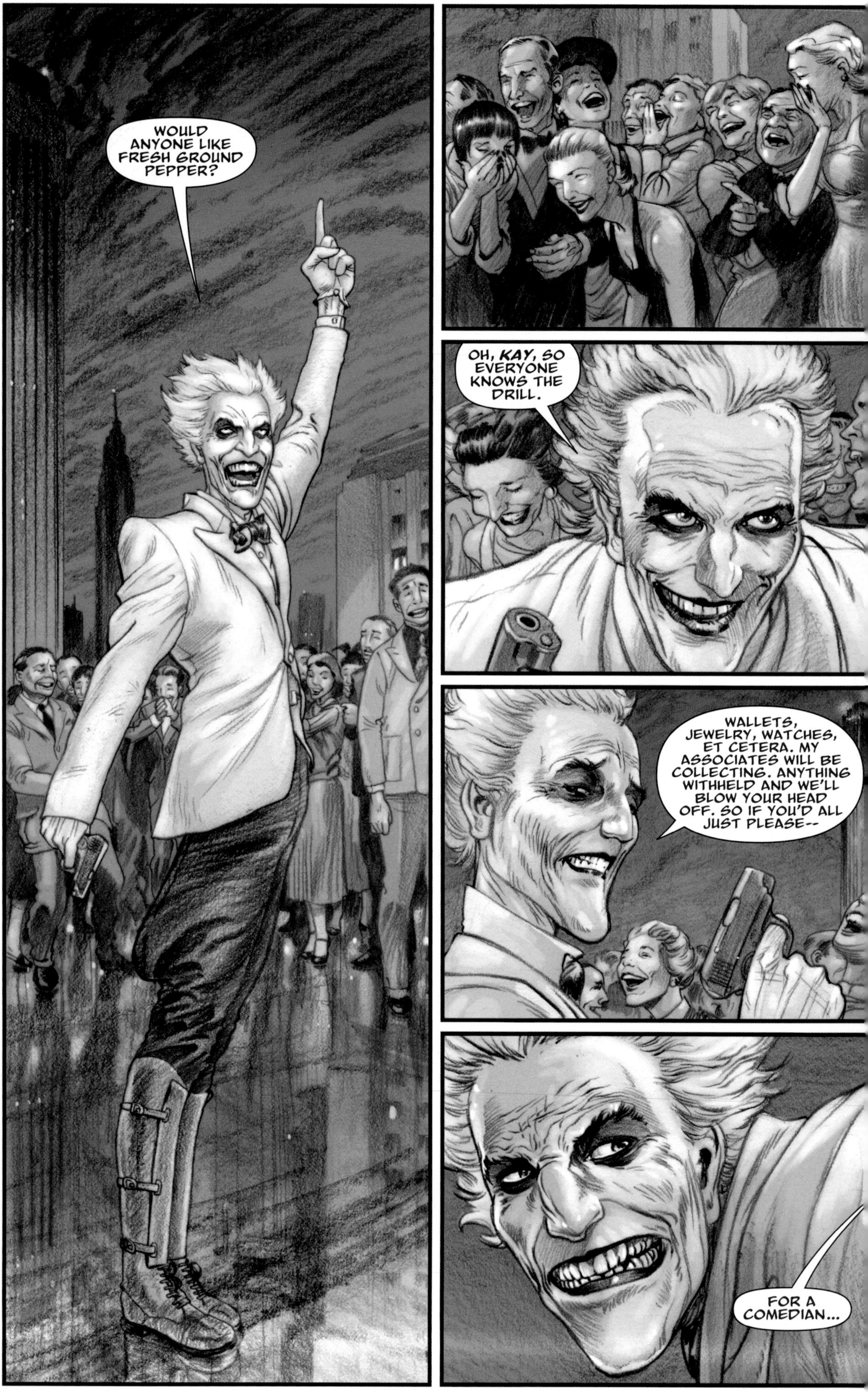

WOULD ANYONE LIKE FRESH GROUND PEPPER?

...YOUR TIMING IS *LOUSY.*

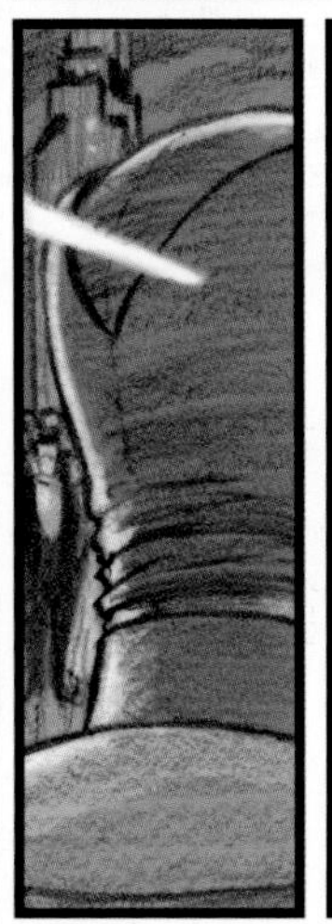

THE STRESSES ON THIS STRUCTURE WERE IMPROPERLY CALCULATED. IT CANNOT SUSTAIN THE WEIGHT. YOU MUST LEAVE IMMEDIATELY!

WHAT?! YOU'RE *MAD*.
OKAY, KIDS...

...GAME-TIME'S OVER.

THIS IS NO GAME. HUNDREDS DEAD ON THE STREET IS NOT SPORT.

OH, I BEG TO DIFFER, FOUR-EYES.

YOU DON'T KNOW *WHAT* YOU'RE TALKING ABOUT. WE CALCULATED *EVERYTHING*.

YOU ARE AN ARROGANT, SELF-ENTITLED WHELP; EASILY INDULGED BY A CORRUPT AND CANCEROUS SYSTEM. AND YOUR OWN POISONOUS VANITY.

HOW *DARE* YOU--

CRRRRRAAAAAAAAAAACCCCCCKKKKKKK!

GRRRRRUUUUUUUUUUCCCCCCKKKKKKK!

I WARNED YOU.

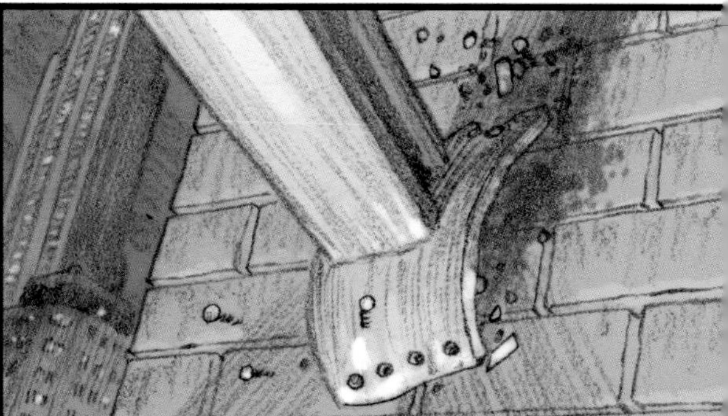

POOM!

THIS WILL BUY US ALL OF TWO MINUTES...

...IF WE'RE LUCKY.
POOM!

OKAY, EVERYONE--

YES! EVERYONE!

HURRY! PULL UP!!

OH, AS IF!
POP!

NEWSFLASH!! REPORTS HAVE JUST COME IN: THE CEILING NIGHTCLUB HAS COLLAPSED AND BROKEN IN TWO, JUST MOMENTS AGO, SENDING PATRONS SCRAMBLING FOR SAFETY AND CROWDS BELOW SCATTERING FOR COVER. ACCORDING TO EYEWITNESS ACCOUNTS, THE BAT-MAN WAS IDENTIFIED AT THE SCENE, AS WELL AS THE NOTORIOUS JOKER, AND A THIRD, AS-YET-UNIDENTIFIED, COSTUMED FIGURE.
ALL WERE APPARENTLY INVOLVED IN THE DESTRUCTION OF THE GLEAMING NEW STRUCTURE, PERCHED HIGH IN THE GOTHAM SKIES. KEM ROOMHAUS, THE ARCHITECTURAL MASTERMIND BEHIND ITS DESIGN, WAS AT THE SCENE AND IS REPORTEDLY UNHARMED. MORE NEWS TO COME AS DETAILS EMERGE FROM THIS ASTONISHING CATASTROPHE. THIS GOTH-I-TONE RADIO NEWS.

DATELINE GOTHAM: LATEST ON SKY-CLUB'S DESTRUCTION:
Initial reports have misidentified the cause of the Ceilin disaster. This reporter was there, testifying that the Joke intended to pillage the club's well-heeled opening-night patrons. In the midst of it, a man with goggles and a personal addres system appeared and proclaimed to the crowd--most of whom were already drugged by a sort of laughing gas--that the structure wa about to collapse and should be evacuated immediately.
This was an alert, not a threat. The stranger declared that the design itself was flawed, and unable to bear the weight of the crowd. This was horrifically borne out. Then the Bat-Man mysteriously arrived, and after a brief confrontation with the Joker (who did not apparently survive) he jury-rigged a cable system that held up the crumbling foundation just long enough to get everyone out. And then vanished, as did the figure in goggles.
What remains to be seen is how this ridiculously conceived structure could have been successfully presented to an astoundingly naive city council, approved with a blind eye by the zoning board, egregiously misconstructed by Gotham Local 27, and then passed inspection. I suspect the real villain here has yet to be revealed. More to come, developing...

RIDICULOUSLY CONCEIVED??!!

ASTOUNDINGLY NAIVE??!!

...EGREGIOUSLY MISCONSTRUCTED...

THE REAL VILLAIN?? THAT CRETIN...

CONGRATULATIONS, KID, THE SWITCHBOARD'S JAMMED. HALF THE CITY WANTS YOUR HEAD. YOU MUST BE DOING SOMETHING RIGHT.

THEY'RE MAD AT *ME*? FOR WHAT, REPORTING WHAT HAPPENED?

YOU DID A LITTLE MORE THAN THAT. *THE SUN, THE NEWS,* AND *THE POST* ARE ALL BLAMING THE WHOLE MESS ON THE FREAKS.

SO...WHY DID YOU LET ME RUN MY PIECE?

BECAUSE I BELIEVE YOU. I THINK YOU'RE RIGHT.

THIS FRANK KID AT THE GAZETTE. WHAT DO WE THINK? DO WE HAVE TO WORRY?

HE'S NOTHING. A SPECK.

GOOD. BUT IF THE SPECK NEEDS TO BE WIPED AWAY...

"WE'RE ON IT."
HELLO, CYNDIA? I...I JUST WANTED TO SEE HOW YOU WERE DOING.

GIGGLE. OH, REALLY. HA-HUMPF.

I DO APOLOGIZE FOR LOSING TRACK OF YOU DURING ALL THE INSANITY.

HEH! WELL, HA-HA! THAT'S WHAT HAPPENS WHEN YOU HIDE UNDER THE TABLECLOTH!! HA-HA!

Dear Mr. Frank,

Please forgive this rather unorthodox method of communication--I cannot afford to be traced, as my identity must remain a secret for the foreseeable future. First, congrats on your ace reportage. You appear to be the single media figure in this city who really seems to understand what's going on. Therefore, I have decided to take a chance and reach out to you with what I have gathered. Enclosed you will find a copy of the original manifest for the crane that collapsed last week. The version of this document currently on file has been altered, to cover up the tracks of those responsible...

As you can see, the crane was never properly supported from the ground. Instead, it was affixed to the roof of the adjacent building, essentially hovering fifteen stories above street level, certainly an accident waiting to happen. Exactly why remains unclear, but if it was the result of a cost-cutting measure, whoever made the call is responsible. As in, whoever altered the manifest. I did not make it to the records department in time to find out who made the switch, but I'd guess it was at the orders of a certain Mr. Bart Loar. You might try asking him about it. If you do, be sure to meet in a public place--I hear he can be murder in private.

More later,

X

INTERESTING. AND TOTALLY INADMISSIBLE.
SIGH. I KNOW. EVEN IF IT'S TRUE--

THERE'S NO WAY TO PROVE IT. OR RESPONSIBLY REPORT IT. THIS LITERALLY HAS "ANONYMOUS NUT JOB" WRITTEN ALL OVER IT.
PROBABLY, BUT...THE MANIFEST ON FILE WITH THE CITY IS WORTH A LOOK,

"DON'T YOU THINK?"
BZZZT
WHAT.
MR. LOAR, OUR SOURCE CALLED. HE SAID TO TELL YOU THE SPECK IS GROWING--THE SPECK WANTS THE MANIFEST PLAN FOR THE CRANE AT GOTHAM SQUARE. AND HE WANTS THE MANIFEST PLAN FOR THE CEILING, TOO.

UNDERSTOOD.
DAMN.

THE SPECK. WIPE HIM.
ROGER THAT.

SPECK IS ASCENDING.
COPY. CLEANUP CREW ON ITS WAY.

MR. FRANK. PLEASE LISTEN TO ME.
BORONA

YOU ARE IN SERIOUS TROUBLE AND I'M HERE TO HELP YOU.

YOU HAVE SIXTY SECONDS, TOPS.

WHO? WHO ARE YOU?
A FRIEND, YOU'RE GOING TO HAVE TO TRUST ME.

WHERE? WHERE ARE YOU?

RAISE THE BLINDS.

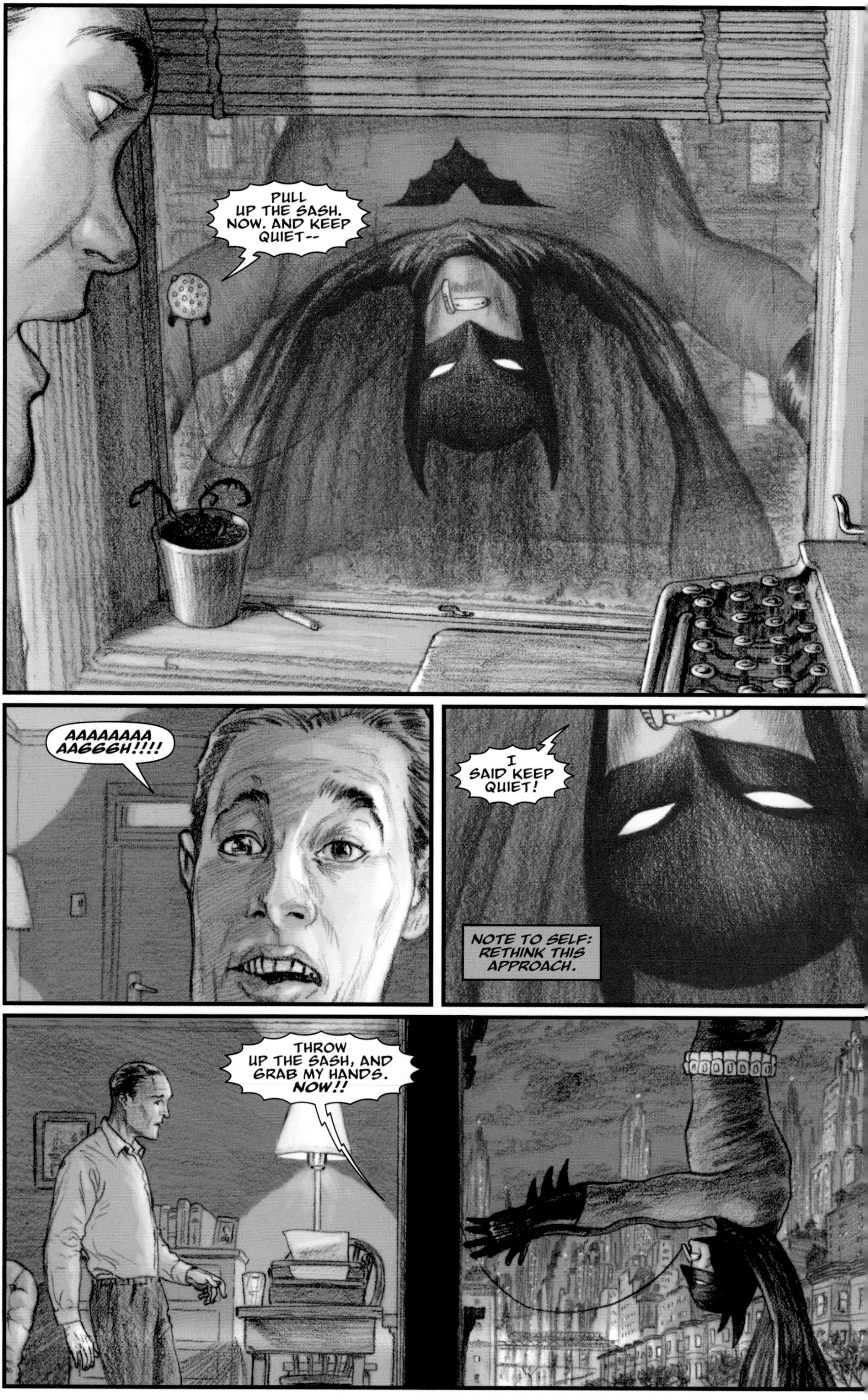

PULL UP THE SASH. NOW. AND KEEP QUIET--

BAM!

ZIPP!

HE WAS *HERE*, I HEARD 'EM! I DON'T LIKE THIS. LET'S BEAT IT.

LET'S TALK.

WHERE HAVE YOU BEEN?!
THINKING. THINGS ARE GETTING... WEIRDER.
TRUST NO ONE.

YOU DON'T KNOW THE HALF OF IT. GUESS WHO'S SUDDENLY DONE A 180 AND HAS DECIDED TO GIVE YOU AN EXCLUSIVE INTERVIEW?
LOAR?
THE SAME.

WELL... THAT'S GREAT, BUT...I DON'T GET IT.

HE WANTS TO SPIN IT, NATCH. DOESN'T MATTER. DO IT BEFORE HE CHANGES HIS MIND.

FOOP!

ABANDON SCHEDULED MEETING WITH BL. RE-PEAT, DO **NOT** KEEP APPT WITH LOAR. CONSIDER THIS WARNING IN YOUR BEST INTEREST X

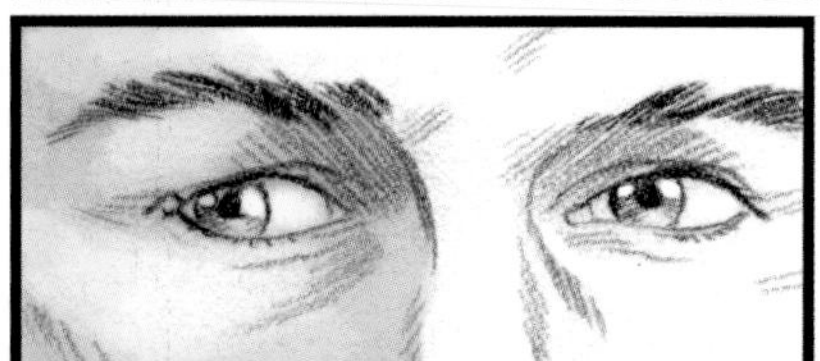

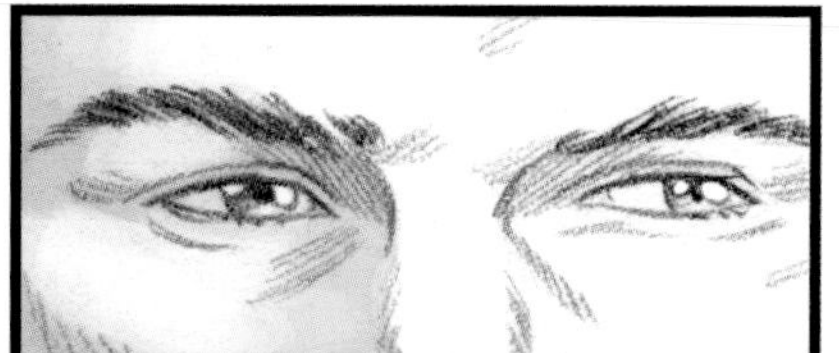

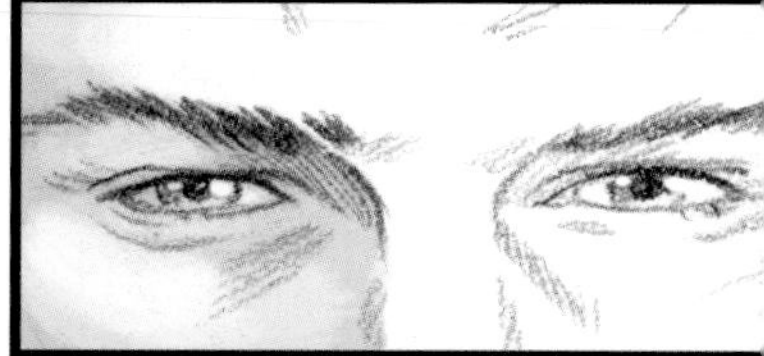

MR. FRANK. GREETINGS.

AFTER YOU.

LET'S GO WHERE WE CAN GET SOME PRIVACY.
CA-CHUNNNG!

SO TELL ME, MR. FRANK...

YEAH, ME. AS OF AN HOUR AGO, I STILL HAVE A JOB.

NO, YOU HAVE A PERCH.
...DO YOU ACTUALLY KNOW ANY WORKING MEN?

...A RAREFIED POST FROM WHICH YOU ARE FREE TO PASS JUDGMENT ON ANYONE AND EVERYTHING YOU SEE FIT...

"...FROM ABOVE IT ALL."

LET ME SHOW YOU SOMETHING.

I MEANT REAL WORKING MEN, WHO BUST THEIR HUMPS FOR AN HONEST DAY'S WAGE. EVERY DAY.

LET ME TELL YOU SOMETHING, KID.
FOUR GENERATIONS OF MY FAMILY BUILT THIS CITY.

THE FIRST ONE DID IT FOR SLAVE WAGES AND AN EARLY GRAVE.
THE SECOND ONE FOUGHT TO ORGANIZE AND SURVIVE.

THE THIRD FIGURED OUT HOW TO UNITE AND THRIVE.
AND THE FOURTH ONE... RULES.

THAT'S VERY...INSPIRING. SO, CAN WE START THE INTERVIEW?

INTERVIEW'S OVER.

WHAT?!!

NOW YOU LISTEN TO ME. I AM GOING BACK DOWN. YOU WILL STAY UP HERE AND THINK LONG AND HARD ABOUT HOW YOU'RE GOING TO PROCEED. UNDERSTAND?
I--

SOMEONE WILL BE BACK HERE AT 6 AM. TO DO A DAY'S HARD WORK. YOU CAN GO THEN. I'M SURE YOU'LL MAKE THE RIGHT DECISION.

HELLO.

YAAAAHHHH!!

MAY I COME IN?

MR. LOAR. LET'S TALK.
NO! NO! YOU--!!

MY, BUT YOU *ARE* AGITATED. WHATEVER'S THE MATTER?

DID I INTERRUPT?
ZZZRRRRRRRRRRKKTT!!

WHAT WAS THAT?!

THAT WAS ME, POWER-WELDING THE DOOR SHUT.

WHY YOU SON-OF-A--

...STRATEGICALLY PLACED, SO THE CRANE WILL TILT AND FALL WEST, DIRECTLY ACROSS THE STREET, INTO THE BUILDING UNDER CONSTRUCTION--BY AN INDEPENDENT CONTRACTOR, AS LUCK WOULD HAVE IT...

...AND THUS RIDDING YOURSELF OF YET ANOTHER INCONVENIENT TRUTHTELLER WHO HAD THE TEMERITY TO GET IN YOUR WAY. AND ALL APPEARING TO BE YET ANOTHER UNFORTUNATE, UNTRACEABLE ACCIDENT. ONE THAT YOU'RE SUPPOSED TO BE WALKING AWAY FROM. RIGHT. NOW.

RRRRRRAAAA AARRRGGGH!!!!!--

WHAM!!

THINK ABOUT WHAT YOU'RE DOING. IT'S MURDER.

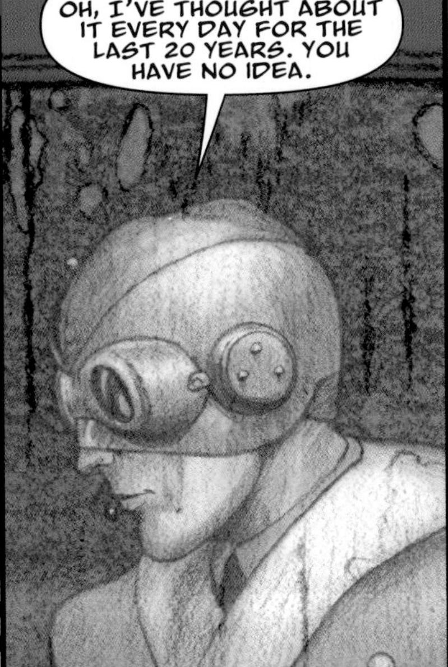
OH, I'VE THOUGHT ABOUT IT EVERY DAY FOR THE LAST 20 YEARS. YOU HAVE NO IDEA.

AND IT'S NOT MURDER. IT'S ASSISTED SUICIDE. THE IRONY IS POSITIVELY SHAKESPEAREAN.

PERHAPS. BUT I CAN'T ALLOW IT TO HAPPEN. HE SHOULD BE TRIED IN A COURT OF LAW.

SAID THE MAN DRESSED AS A GARGOYLE SO HE CAN DO WHATEVER HE WANTS. YOU ARE ONE STRANGE, INTERESTING PERSON. I WOULD HAVE ENJOYED TALKING MORE WITH YOU.
ANYWAY, NO. NO, WE ALL KNOW THEY TRIED THAT ALREADY, SO TO SPEAK. HE'D JUST BUY HIS WAY OUT OF IT AGAIN. OR THREATEN TO HAVE THE JURORS' CHILDREN DISAPPEAR. OR ORDER THE JUDGE'S CAR BLOWN UP.

NO, MR. LOAR. TIME'S UP.

AREN'T YOU FORGETTING SOMETHING?

I'D BETTER NOT BE.

YOU'RE TRAPPED UP HERE WITH US. ACCORDING TO WHAT YOU'VE SAID, YOU WON'T HAVE TIME TO ESCAPE.

OH, THAT. YES, THAT WOULD BE TRUE...

...IF I WERE ACTUALLY HERE.

BWIPP

ZZZZZZZZT!

WELL, MR. "EXACTO", I MUST SAY...
POOM!

...IF YOU WEREN'T TRYING SO HARD TO KILL ME...

...I'D HIRE YOU.
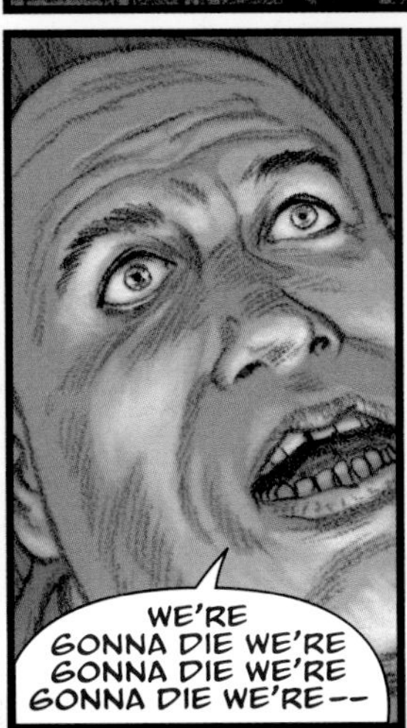
WE'RE GONNA DIE WE'RE GONNA DIE WE'RE GONNA DIE WE'RE--

SHUT UP!!
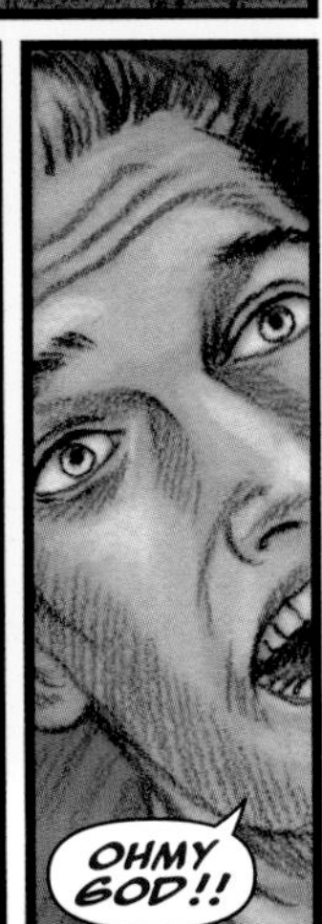
OHMY GOD!!

WHAT'S THAT??
IT'S A--

BOOOOM

OKAY, HERE WE...
TWENTY SECONDS AGO.

WHAT'S THAT?!!

IT'S A PROTO-TYPE.

A PROTOTYPE OF WHAT?! WE'RE GONNA DIE! WE'REGONNADIEWE'REGONNA DIEWE'REGONNADIEWE'RE

SHUT UP!!

FIVE SECONDS AGO.
LISTEN TO ME! THIS IS AN IMPACT NEUTRALIZER, IT EMITS A STASIS FIELD!

FOUR SECONDS...
I'VE NEVER TESTED IT!

THREE...
STAY AS CLOSE TO ME AS YOU CAN! IT'LL EITHER WORK...

TWO...
...OR IT WON--

NOW.

UHNNNN...
WELL, IT WORKS.

SORT OF.

THEY'RE BOTH BREATHING, PULSES CHECK. FRANK DOESN'T SEEM TOO BAD. LOAR, HARDER TO TELL. I DON'T LIKE THE WAY HIS PUPILS ARE DILATED...

OH, GREAT.
LOOK! IT'S THE BAT-MAN!! DON'T MOVE!

HALT! YOU'RE UNDER ARREST!

POLICE
SO MUCH FOR MY PUBLIC IMAGE...

BAT-MAN AT SCENE OF LATEST CRANE COLLAPSE

Pattern Suspected

Two Victims Found Unconscious.
Union Boss Critical.

'TWOULD APPEAR YOU NEED A NEW PRESS AGENT, SIR.

I KEEP REPLAYING IT IN MY HEAD. THIS EXACTO GUY, THIS WAS MORE THAN SOME MORAL CRUSADE FOR HIM. IT WAS PERSONAL. HE SAID HE'D BEEN WAITING 20 YEARS TO GET LOAR.

I WOULD SAY THAT SOUNDS RATHER FAMILIAR.

SO THE QUESTION IS, WHO HAS A BIG ENOUGH BEEF WITH BART LOAR TO WANT HIM DEAD?
TAPPITY-TAP-TAP-TAP

CALCULATING POTENTIAL CANDIDATES FOR ASSASSINATION OF BART LOAR, PRESIDENT, GOTHAM LOCAL 27.
BASED ON RECORDED DISPUTES, BOTH PUBLIC AND PRIVATE, WITH MANAGEMENT, EMPLOYEES, PERSONAL RELATIONS, CLERGY, ILLICIT LIAISONS, ETC.
RESULTS: 3,742
SIGH.

IT WASN'T EASY TO GET A GOOD LOOK AT HIM THROUGH THE GLASS, BUT EXACTO DIDN'T SEEM OLD ENOUGH TO HAVE A 20-YEAR GRUDGE AGAINST ANYONE. UNLESS...

HE'S BEEN HARBORING IT SINCE HE WAS A CHILD.

TWENTY YEARS AGO
GREENSIDE ARCHITECTS, INC. GREGOR GREENSIDE, PROPRIETOR, IS ENGAGED IN CONVERSATION WITH HIS WIFE, AUDREY.
I, I SUPPOSE THIS IS GOOD-BYE.

DID YOU HEAR ME?

LOUD AND CLEAR. DON'T SLAM THE DOOR.

THAT, THAT'S IT?

WELL THAT'S WHAT YOU WANTED, NO?

WHAT I WANTED?
NO. NOT BEFORE.
BUT IT IS NOW.

WELL THEN, THIS MUST BE YOUR LUCKY DAY.

OH, BART...
HEY, BABY. THAT EVERYTHING? DRY THOSE TEARS, BABY...
SANDWICH SHOP

GARNETT, AREN'T YOU SUPPOSED TO BE IN SCHOOL?

I'M ***SO*** BORED. THOSE KIDS STILL CAN'T EVEN ***READ*** YET. IT'S A JOKE. I TURNED IN THIS WEEK'S ASSIGNMENTS AND GOT A BATHROOM PASS.

UNDERSTOOD. I'LL THINK OF SOMETHING TO SAY TO THE SCHOOL. AGAIN.
SHARPEN ALL OF THE HB PENCILS. AND PULL UP THE WAYNE STATION PLANS. THERE'S WORK TO DO.

YES, SIR.

TODAY.
WHAT ARE YOU DOING HERE?

WHAT ARE YOU DOING HERE?

WHAT THE HECK?

BZZZT

GREENSIDE ARCHITECTS INC.
UM, HELLO?

HELLO, MY NAME IS CYNDIA SYL, I NEED TO --

HAVE A SEAT.

THE, AH, DOOR. THAT'S RATHER OFF-PUTTING, DON'T YOU THINK?

YES, WELL, THAT WAS DAD'S LITMUS TEST FOR EVERYONE, INCLUDING HIMSELF. EVERY MORNING, WHEN HE GOT HERE TO WORK, THAT WAS THE QUESTION WE REALLY SHOULD BE ASKING OUR-SELVES ALL THE TIME. SO, MISS SYL--

WHAT ARE YOU DOING HERE?

WELL, I.
I'M TRYING TO FIND YOUR FATHER.

JOIN THE CLUB. I'VE TOLD EVERYTHING I KNOW TO THE POLICE. FOR ALL THE GOOD *THAT* WILL DO.

BUT AREN'T YOU WORRIED?

MISS SYL, I'VE BEEN WORRYING ABOUT GREGOR SINCE THE DAY I WAS BORN. IT'S MY NATURAL STATE. WHETHER HE'S HERE OR NOT.

BUT I-- OH. WHAT IS THAT?

WHAT?

OH, THAT.

THAT'S SOMETHING I DEVELOPED WITH DAD. WE CALL IT A SMART PROJECTION SYSTEM. IT CAN SEND A REAL-TIME THREE-DIMENSIONAL PROJECTION ANYWHERE YOU WANT, AS LONG AS YOU HAVE THE COORDINATES. WE CREATED IT TO PRESENT LARGE 3-D ARCHITECTURAL MODELS TO CLIENTS TOO FAR AWAY TO VISIT.

NOT THAT WE'VE EVER HAD ANY.

SO, IF I MAY ASK, HOW IS BUSINESS?

DO YOU KNOW WHAT WE'VE BEEN PAYING THE BILLS WITH, AFTER THE DISGRACE OF WAYNE CENTRAL STATION?
SHEDS AND DOGHOUSES. FOR YEARS. LITERALLY. OH, THE POWER OF WORD-OF-MOUTH.

YOU CAN'T BE SERIOUS.

OH, SERIOUS AS A CANCER. CAN I ASK YOU SOMETHING?
OF COURSE.

WE'VE APPRECIATED YOUR EFFORTS ON BEHALF OF THE STATION, VERY MUCH. BUT WHY WAIT 'TIL NOW TO CONTACT US, TO VISIT?

THAT'S FAIR ENOUGH, I SUPPOSE.
I WAS, WELL, SCARED.

SCARED? OF WHAT?

OF YOUR FATHER'S GENIUS.

YOU CAN JOIN THAT CLUB TOO.
SO YOU REALLY HAVE NO IDEA WHERE HE IS?

"NONE. HE CERTAINLY ISN'T AT HOME."
MA'AM.

FLICK!

HELLO, CYNDIA.

SCREAM.

GOTHAM MEMORIAL HOSPITAL, ICU.
WHAT'S MR. LOAR'S PROGNOSIS?
HARD TO SAY. HE WAS A HEAVY SMOKER, CRUCIAL ARTERIES NEARLY BLOCKED, DOESN'T HELP. HE COULD SNAP OUT OF IT AT ANY TIME. OR NOT.

AND HOW ABOUT MR. FRANK?
SEE FOR YOURSELF.

TAP-TAP-TAP
DING!

EXCELLENT. I DON'T WANT TO DISTURB HIM.
BRIIP!
ALFRED.

SIR. JUST REMINDING YOU OF YOUR LUNCH DATE WITH MISS SYL.
OH, DON'T WORRY...

"...I DIDN'T FORGET."
MR. WAYNE, A CALL FOR YOU, SIR.

MR. WAYNE, I'M SORRY TO BOTHER YOU, BUT THIS IS MISS SYL'S SOCIAL SECRETARY. IS SHE THERE?
NO. AS A MATTER OF FACT, I--
WELL, THAT'S PROBABLY BECAUSE...

SHE'S WITH ME.

NO!! YOU--

LISTEN GOOD AND QUICK: GO HOME. YOU WILL RECEIVE FURTHER ORDERS SHORTLY. IF YOU MAKE ANY ATTEMPT TO CONTACT THE POLICE OR THAT FLYING RAT, HER TIME IS UP.

HELLO, MISS SYL'S RESIDENCE.
OH, HI THERE. THIS IS BRUCE WAYNE CALLING. IS MISS SYL THERE?
AS A MATTER OF FACT, NO, MR. WAYNE. SHE HAS AN APPOINTMENT TO MEET YOU FOR LUNCH. BUT NO ONE'S SEEN HER HERE TODAY, IT'S A LITTLE STRANGE.
I SEE. HMM, COULD YOU TELL ME WHERE HER LAST APPOINTMENT WAS YESTERDAY?
OKAY, LET'S SEE HERE. IT WAS AT...

"...GREENSIDE ARCHITECTS."
WHAT ARE YOU DOING HERE?
BAM
BAM
BAM

JEEZ LOUISE, WAIT-A--
ARE YOU
G HERE?

WHOA.

I UNDERSTAND CYNDIA SYL WAS HERE LAST NIGHT.
YES. SHE'S AN AMAZING GIRL. VERY SMART.
DID SHE INDICATE AT ALL WHY SHE MADE A VISIT?

MR. WAYNE, I HARDLY NEED TO REMIND YOU OF HER PASSIONS REGARDING THE WC STATION.
SHE WANTED TO KNOW IF I HAD ANY INFORMATION ON MY FATHER'S WHEREABOUTS. PERIOD.

AND DO YOU?

ARE YOU
HERE?
NO, AS I TOLD HER. BUT I SUSPECT THE WORST.
WHY?

MR. WAYNE, I'LL BE BLUNT. DO YOU HAVE ANY IDEA WHAT IT TAKES TO GET SOMETHING BUILT IN THIS CITY?

"DO YOU HAVE ANY IDEA WHAT HAPPENED?"
TWENTY YEARS AGO
GREENSIDE. WHAT THE HELL IS THIS?
WHAT ARE YOU DOING HERE?

THAT IS A LIGHTING FIXTURE BY IACONE INC., FROM MILAN, MR. LOAR. IT LOOKS FINE AND USES A THIRD OF THE ELECTRICITY OF U.S. FIXTURES. IT WILL BE INSTALLED IN EVERY OFFICE SPACE AND LAVATORY OF THE BUILDING.

MR. GREENSIDE, NEED I TELL YOU, THIS IS NOT UNION-APPROVED.
YOU
RE?

THEN GET IT APPROVED, MR. LOAR, THAT IS YOUR JOB.

THE NEXT MORNING.
UH, MR. GREENSIDE, SOMETHING'S HAPPENED.

SPEAK.
ALL OF, WELL, ALL OF THE TOILETS AT THE WORK SITE--ALL 200-PLUS OF THEM--HAVE DEVELOPED A SEVERE CRACK. OVERNIGHT.

THEY ALL NEED TO BE REPLACED. IF I... IF I DIDN'T KNOW BETTER, SIR, I'D SAY SOMEONE HIT EACH ONE OF THEM, HARD, WITH A BALL-PEEN HAMMER, SIR. BUT THAT'S JUST MY OPINION. SIR.

WHAT IN *GOD'S NAME* IS GOING ON HERE?!!
B. LOA
CHIEF

REAL SHAME ABOUT THE TOILETS, MR. G. THOSE SUDDEN TREMORS CAN BE MURDER.
SAY, ANY MORE THOUGHTS ON THAT LIGHTING FIXTURE? HAVEN'T ORDERED IT YET.

WHY YOU *VENOMOUS* LITTLE--

NOW NOW, MR. GREENSIDE. THERE'S NO NEED FOR THAT.

AND SAY, HOW'S THAT BOY OF YOURS? HE STILL WALK TO SCHOOL?

OKAY, SO *TAKE* THAT EXAMPLE AND APPLY IT TO EVERY ASPECT OF THE BUILDING: THE INADEQUATE MORTAR GRADE, THE SHODDY BUTTRESSING, THE SKIMPING ON THE FOUNDATION, AND SO ON.
IT WAS IN BART LOAR'S BEST INTEREST THAT THE WAYNE CENTRAL STATION WOULD LAST SCARCELY TEN YEARS. THEN TEAR IT DOWN AND REDO IT. JUST AS BADLY, IF HE COULD GET AWAY WITH IT.

WHY, *WHY* WASN'T MY FATHER *TOLD*?!

YOUR FATHER WAS DEAD.

OKAY, WHY?

OH, SWEETIE, IF YOU WEREN'T ABOUT TO DIE, WE COULD BOND! I SAW YOU AT THE CEILING. YOU WERE WORKING IT, BABE-A-LICIOUS. YOU DEFINITELY CAUGHT THE BAT-BOOB'S EYE.

LIKE YOU DIDN'T NOTICE: ONCE THINGS FELL APART, YOU WERE PRIORITY ONE.
REALLY?
OH, NO QUESTION. WHAT, IS LOVE BLIND, OR JUST DUMB? WHICHEVER, YOU'RE THE BAIT. LIVE WITH IT.

"OR THE OPPOSITE, AS THE CASE MAY BE."
MR. WAYNE, WITH ALL DUE RESPECT, YOU WATCHED YOUR FATHER DIE IN A SINGLE INSTANT. I CAN ONLY IMAGINE HOW DEVASTATING THAT WAS. FOR ME IT'S THE OPPOSITE: SINCE GREGOR WAS FORCED TO COMPROMISE ON THE WAYNE CENTRAL STATION, ONLY TO HAVE IT CONDEMNED BECAUSE OF THOSE VERY COMPROMISES, I'VE BEEN WATCHING HIM DIE IN SLOW MOTION, SECOND BY GRUELING SECOND, FOR OVER TWO DECADES.

GARNETT, WHY DIDN'T GREGOR GO TO THE AUTHORITIES?

MR. WAYNE, DO I EVEN NEED TO TELL YOU? BART LOAR *WAS* THE AUTHORITY. HE *IS* THE AUTHORITY.

GARNETT, THAT *CAN* CHANGE, I--
BRRRPT!

I--I'M SORRY. IRONICALLY, I HAVE A MEETING AT MY OFFICE IN TWENTY MINUTES WITH ROOMHAUS, ABOUT THE FINAL PHASE OF THE NEW STATION DESIGN. I DON'T SUPPOSE YOU'D LIKE TO ATTEND?

AS A MATTER OF FACT, NO. I WOULD NOT.
MR. WAYNE, ABOUT MISS SYL--IS SHE ALL RIGHT?

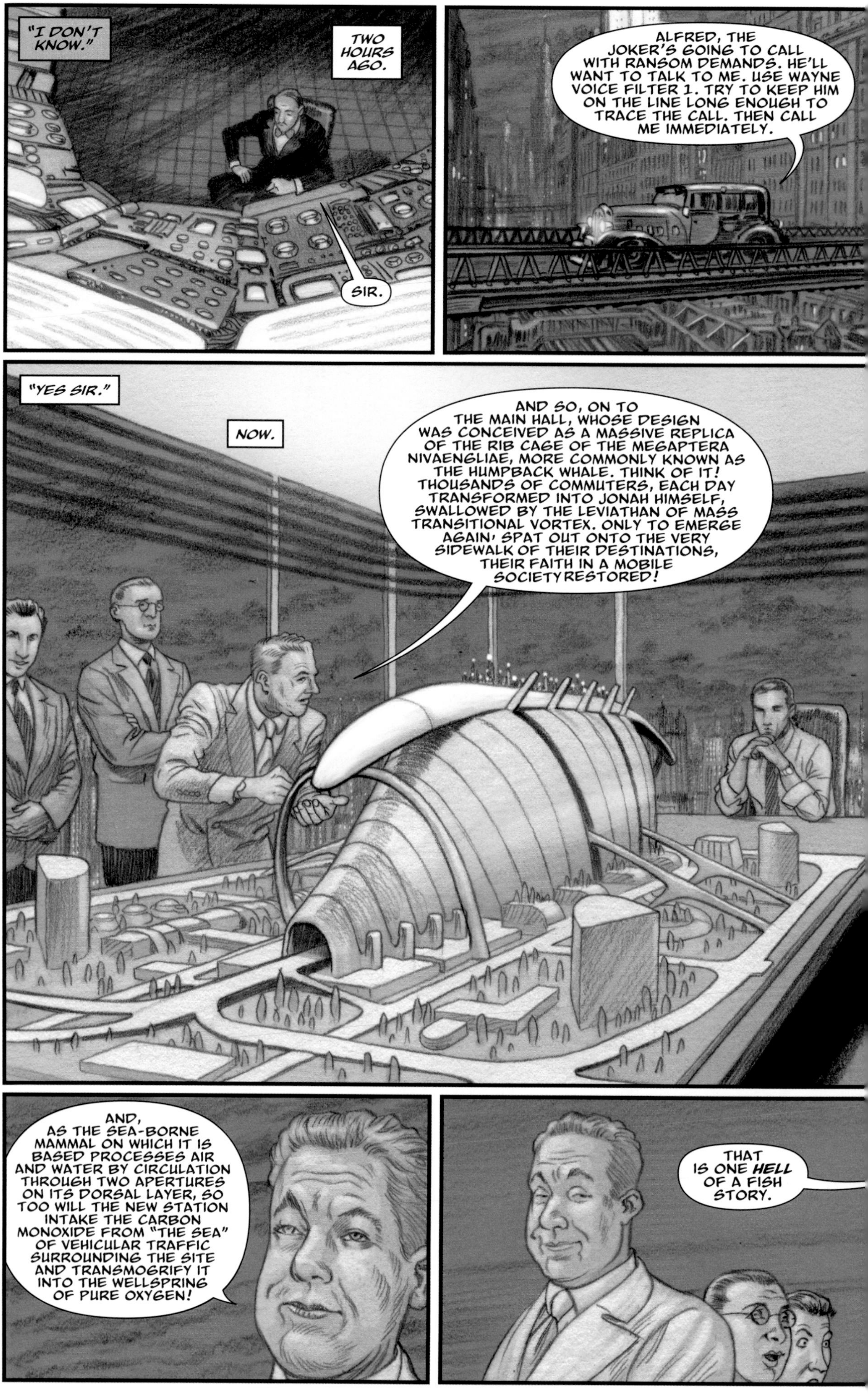

"I DON'T KNOW."
TWO HOURS AGO.
SIR.

ALFRED, THE JOKER'S GOING TO CALL WITH RANSOM DEMANDS. HE'LL WANT TO TALK TO ME. USE WAYNE VOICE FILTER 1. TRY TO KEEP HIM ON THE LINE LONG ENOUGH TO TRACE THE CALL. THEN CALL ME IMMEDIATELY.

"YES SIR."

NOW.

AND SO, ON TO THE MAIN HALL, WHOSE DESIGN WAS CONCEIVED AS A MASSIVE REPLICA OF THE RIB CAGE OF THE MEGAPTERA NIVAENGLIAE, MORE COMMONLY KNOWN AS THE HUMPBACK WHALE. THINK OF IT! THOUSANDS OF COMMUTERS, EACH DAY TRANSFORMED INTO JONAH HIMSELF, SWALLOWED BY THE LEVIATHAN OF MASS TRANSITIONAL VORTEX. ONLY TO EMERGE AGAIN, SPAT OUT ONTO THE VERY SIDEWALK OF THEIR DESTINATIONS, THEIR FAITH IN A MOBILE SOCIETY RESTORED!

AND, AS THE SEA-BORNE MAMMAL ON WHICH IT IS BASED PROCESSES AIR AND WATER BY CIRCULATION THROUGH TWO APERTURES ON ITS DORSAL LAYER, SO TOO WILL THE NEW STATION INTAKE THE CARBON MONOXIDE FROM "THE SEA" OF VEHICULAR TRAFFIC SURROUNDING THE SITE AND TRANSMOGRIFY IT INTO THE WELLSPRING OF PURE OXYGEN!

THAT IS ONE ***HELL*** OF A FISH STORY.

YOU!
MR. ROOMHAUS, WE BOTH KNOW THAT CONVERTING THE CO_2 FROM THE CAR EXHAUST USING THE IONIZATION PROCESSOR SPECCED IN YOUR PLANS WOULD NEVER WORK THE WAY YOU DESCRIBE. YOU'RE MISLEADING YOUR CLIENT.
HOW DARE YOU! GET IN HERE AND FACE ME!
OH, I'LL JUST STAY OUT HERE, THANK YOU, FLOATING MYSTERIOUSLY.

I **KNEW** HE WOULDN'T BE ABLE TO RESIST. THIS IS STARTING TO MAKE SENSE, BUT HOW DOES THE JOKER FIT INTO IT?
AND YOU ARE?
IT DOESN'T MATTER WHO I AM. WHAT MATTERS IS THAT THIS MAN IS SELLING YOU A BILL OF GOODS. AND YOU'RE BUYING. DIDN'T THE CEILING TEACH YOU ANYTHING?

YOU WALL-EYED **WORM**!!

I HAVE TO SAY, UNDER THE PRESENT CIRCUMSTANCES YOU'RE NOT PRESENTING THE MOST COMPELLING CASE.
THEN CONSIDER THIS. CHECK THE FILES: YOUR FATHER'S ORIGINAL ARCHITECT TRIED TO DO THE SAME THING. IT DIDN'T WORK THEN, EITHER.

BZZZZT!

ALFRED. DID YOU GET THE SIGNAL?
I BELIEVE SO, SIR. AS YOU SUSPECTED, BOTH EXACTO AND THE JOKER ARE OPERATING OUT OF THE OLD CENTRAL STATION.

IS THE LAUNCH ACTIVATED AND READY?
YES, SIR. AT YOUR COMMAND.
EXCELLENT. ON MY WAY. DEBRIEF ME IN THE ELEVATOR.

MR. ROOMHAUS, YOU'LL EXCUSE ME. PACK UP. ESTHER WILL SEE YOU OUT.

CLICK
OKAY ALFRED, WE'RE CLEAR. DETAILS.

I WISH I HAD MORE TO TELL YOU, SIR. THE JOKER WANTS $5 MILLION FROM MR. WAYNE BY MIDNIGHT OR MISS SYL DIES, AND HE'LL BRING DOWN THE WHOLE STRUCTURE. BUT THERE SEEMS TO BE MORE TO IT.

WHY?
THE DROP-OFF POINT IS MILES FROM WHERE HE IS ACTUALLY LOCATED, AND I DON'T DETECT ANYONE IN THE AREA WAITING FOR IT.

ALFRED, WHERE IN THE BUILDING IS THE SIGNAL COMING FROM?

FROM THE TOP FLOOR, SIR.

"PERFECT."
CLICK!
HUUUUMMM
ZWOOORRRM
WHUP WHUP
WHUP WHUP
"AND EXACTO, WHAT'S THAT STORY?"
"HARDER TO DETERMINE, SIR. HE'S BROADCASTING HIS IMAGE FROM SOMEWHERE WITHIN THE SAME BUILDING, BUT AT A LOWER FREQUENCY. POSSIBLY IN THE DEPTHS OF AN ABANDONED SUBWAY STOP."

WELL, HELLO.

IT'S BEEN QUITE THE EVENTFUL NIGHT.

⋟HUFF⋞
MR. GREENSIDE? IS THAT YOU? WHAT IS THIS ROOM?
IT IS MY COVERT SANCTUM.

I HAD IT BUILT IN SECRET, WHEN I DREW UP THE FIRST PLANS. IT'S TO BE MY FINAL RESTING PLACE.
I SHOULD TELL YOU: GARNETT THINKS YOU'RE JAMES GORDON, OR HARVEY DENT. OR EVEN THE MAYOR. SOMEONE WHO REALLY WANTS TO GET SOMETHING DONE IN THIS TOWN.

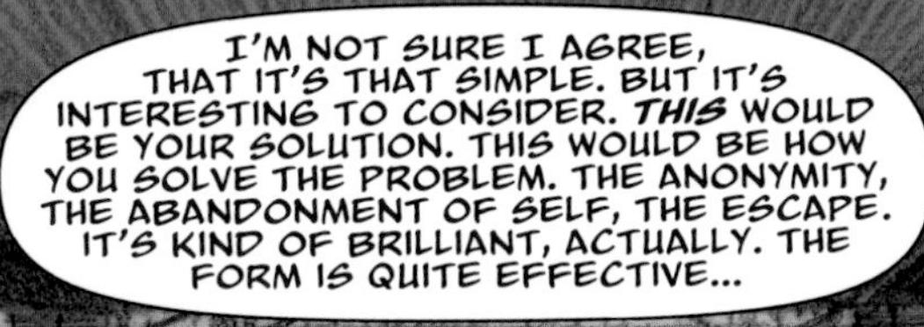
I'M NOT SURE I AGREE, THAT IT'S THAT SIMPLE. BUT IT'S INTERESTING TO CONSIDER. THIS WOULD BE YOUR SOLUTION. THIS WOULD BE HOW YOU SOLVE THE PROBLEM. THE ANONYMITY, THE ABANDONMENT OF SELF, THE ESCAPE. IT'S KIND OF BRILLIANT, ACTUALLY. THE FORM IS QUITE EFFECTIVE...

AND THE CONTENT, WELL. NO ONE'S SUPPOSED TO KNOW WHAT THAT IS, ARE THEY? HEH-HEH.

MR. GREENSIDE, WE'VE GOT TO MOVE. I BELIEVE THE JOKER IS GOING TO BRING THIS WHOLE PLACE DOWN.

OH, I'M COUNTING ON IT. YOU HAVE YOUR SOLUTION, I HAVE MINE. THIS BUILDING AND I...
WE BELONG DEAD.
NO!!
CA-CHUNG!

KA-WHAMM!

KRRASH!
KRASH!

WHOOOMP!

LET ME GUESS: YOU'RE ACTUALLY HERE.

HUKK! WAIT! BEFORE YOU HIT ME, LISTEN! YOU HAVE ME HOPELESSLY OUTCLASSED IN TERMS OF STRENGTH, AGILITY AND COMBAT SKILL. BUT THERE'S ONE THING I HAVE OVER YOU.

MAKE IT QUICK.
IN--IN ORDER TO SURVIVE, I-I WILL KILL YOU.
DO YOU HAVE ANY IDEA HOW MANY TIMES I'VE HEARD THA--
BWUP!

I WARNED YOU! ARE YOU OKAY? I DIDN'T WANT TO--

OKAY, WHERE WERE WE?
GUURRK!!

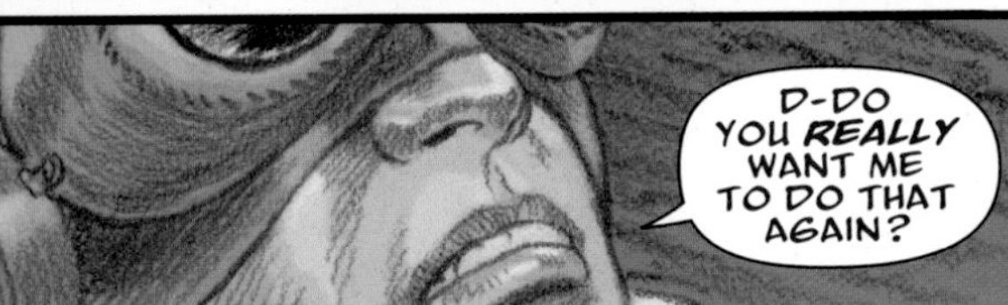
D-DO YOU *REALLY* WANT ME TO DO THAT AGAIN?

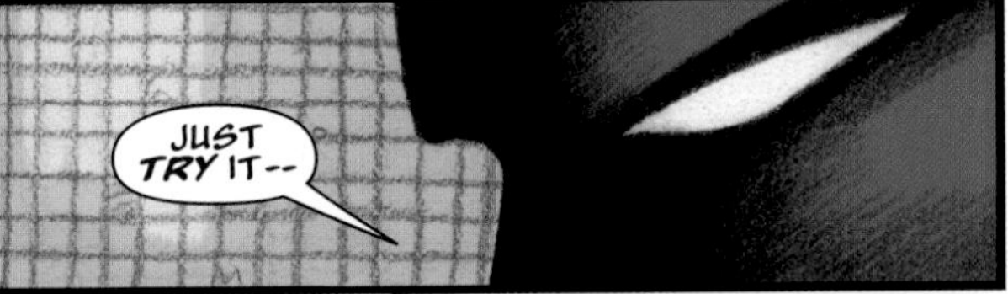
JUST *TRY* IT--

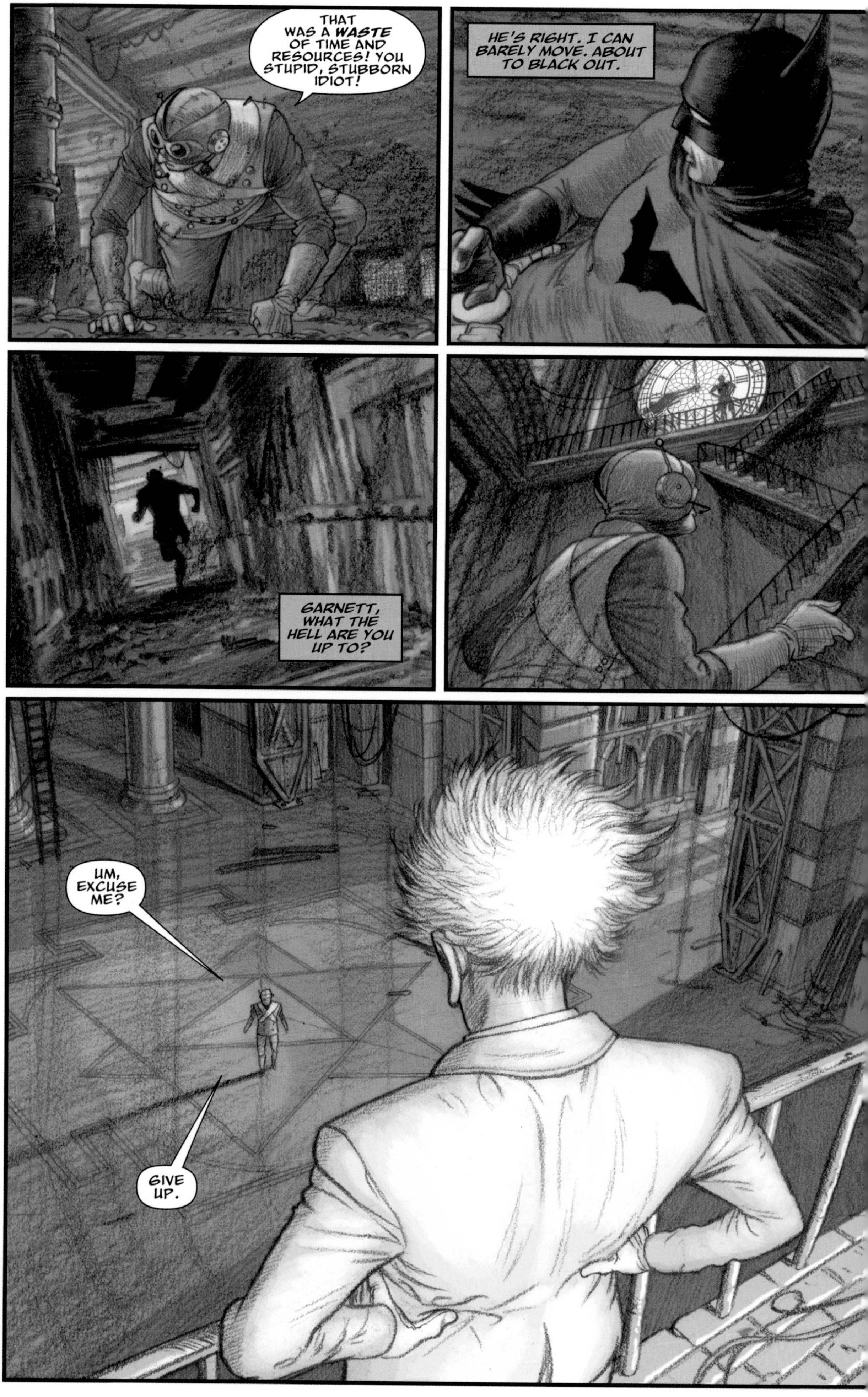

THAT WAS A *WASTE* OF TIME AND RESOURCES! YOU STUPID, STUBBORN IDIOT!

HE'S RIGHT. I CAN BARELY MOVE. ABOUT TO BLACK OUT.

GARNETT, WHAT THE HELL ARE YOU UP TO?

UM, EXCUSE ME?
GIVE UP.

WHO THE HELL ARE YOU, AND WHY SHOULD I GIVE A DAMN?

UH, BECAUSE I HAVE YOUR IGNITION DEVICE. SO COME ON DOWN. YOU'RE NOT DOING THIS RIGHT. LET'S DISCUSS.

WHAT? HOW DID YOU--

MISS SYL. WE MUST ACT QUICKLY. OH MY GOD.

OKAY, WHELP. SHOW YOURSELF. IF YOU DARE.
WHAT?

IT'S ALL SO EASY, ISN'T IT?
TICK TICK TICK TICK TICK TICK

SCARE A GIRL HALF TO DEATH, KIDNAP HER, TIE HER TO A CLOCK, WITH A KNIFE AT THE FINISH LINE.
TICK TICK TICK

AND ALL JUST SO YOU CAN GET THE ATTENTION OF THE BAT-MAN.
WHY, YOU BIG, BAD BRUISER, YOU.
TICK TICK

WELL NOW, THAT'S SOME LITTLE MOUTH ON YOU, GIRLEEN. I MAY JUST HAVE TO KEEP IT FOR A SOUVENIR.
TICK TICK TICK

YES, I SUPPOSE YOU COULD...
TICK

...IF I WERE ACTUALLY HERE.
TICK TICK TICK

BZZZZT!!
DING!

WHERE IS SHE?!!!

HONESTLY, WOULD YOU BELIEVE YOU'RE ASKING THE WRONG PERSON?

YOU SHOULDN'T HAVE DONE THAT.

YOU PULLED THE TRIGGER.

BAAAA-WOOOOOM!!!

HHAHAHAHAHAH

HOLD ON! I'M ALMOST--

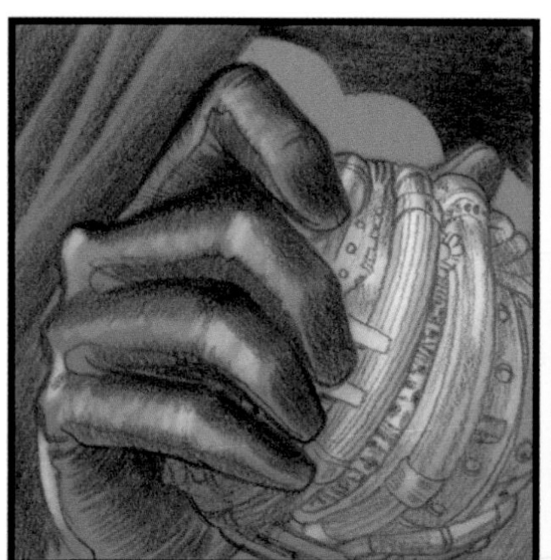

OH MY GOD, OH MY GOD. I, I...

HOW ARE YOUR LEGS?
UM, SORT OF OKAY? I THINK.

RUN.

DATELINE, GOTHAM: The saga of the Wayne Central Station is finally over, at least for now. By all accounts, there were no casualties as a result of its mysterious demolition last night. Unless you consider the building itself. It will be missed, by this reporter and by the thousands of wide-eyed Gothamites who passed through its magnificent spaces every day. Despite its considerable flaws, it represented the gateway to their hopes and dreams.
All of us in this troubled city can surely agree: only something just as extraordinary could possibly replace what has been lost. We eagerly await whatever it is. May it rise soon on our future's horizon.

HI.

DARLING, I'D JUST HEARD THAT NO LESS THAN THE BAT-MAN DELIVERED YOU HERE THIS MORNING.

HMPF. IS THAT WHY YOU'RE HERE... TO TELL ME *THAT*?

SWEETNESS, YOU'RE GOING TO HAVE TO CEASE ALL THIS ADVENTURING. IT'S SIMPLY NOT LADYLIKE.

ACTUALLY, NO. I SEEM TO BE MISSING A BUILDING. SO...

DO YOU REALLY MEAN IT?

OH, I MEAN IT. HEY, KNOW ANYONE WHO'D BE INTERESTED IN BEING CHIEF CONSULTANT?

YOU'RE LOOKING AT HER.
MR. WAYNE, YOU'RE MY HERO.

MR. GREENSIDE, YOU'RE HIRED.
EXCUSE ME, MR. WAYNE? HIRED TO DO WHAT?

TO REDESIGN WAYNE CENTRAL STATION. WHY DON'T YOU ADAPT YOUR FATHER'S DESIGN, THE WAY IT WAS SUPPOSED TO BE IN THE FIRST PLACE?
AND I'LL GET IT BUILT.
WE'LL DO IT RIGHT THIS TIME. FOR THEM. FOR THE CITY.

I CAN'T BELIEVE IT. I MEAN, THIS IS... WHEN DO WE START?

YESTERDAY. YOU'LL HAVE A STAFF. CYNDIA SYL WILL BE YOUR POINT PERSON. WE'LL FIGURE IT OUT. MY PERSONAL SCHEDULE TENDS TO BE ERRATIC.

TWO WEEKS FROM NOW.
HOLD STILL.

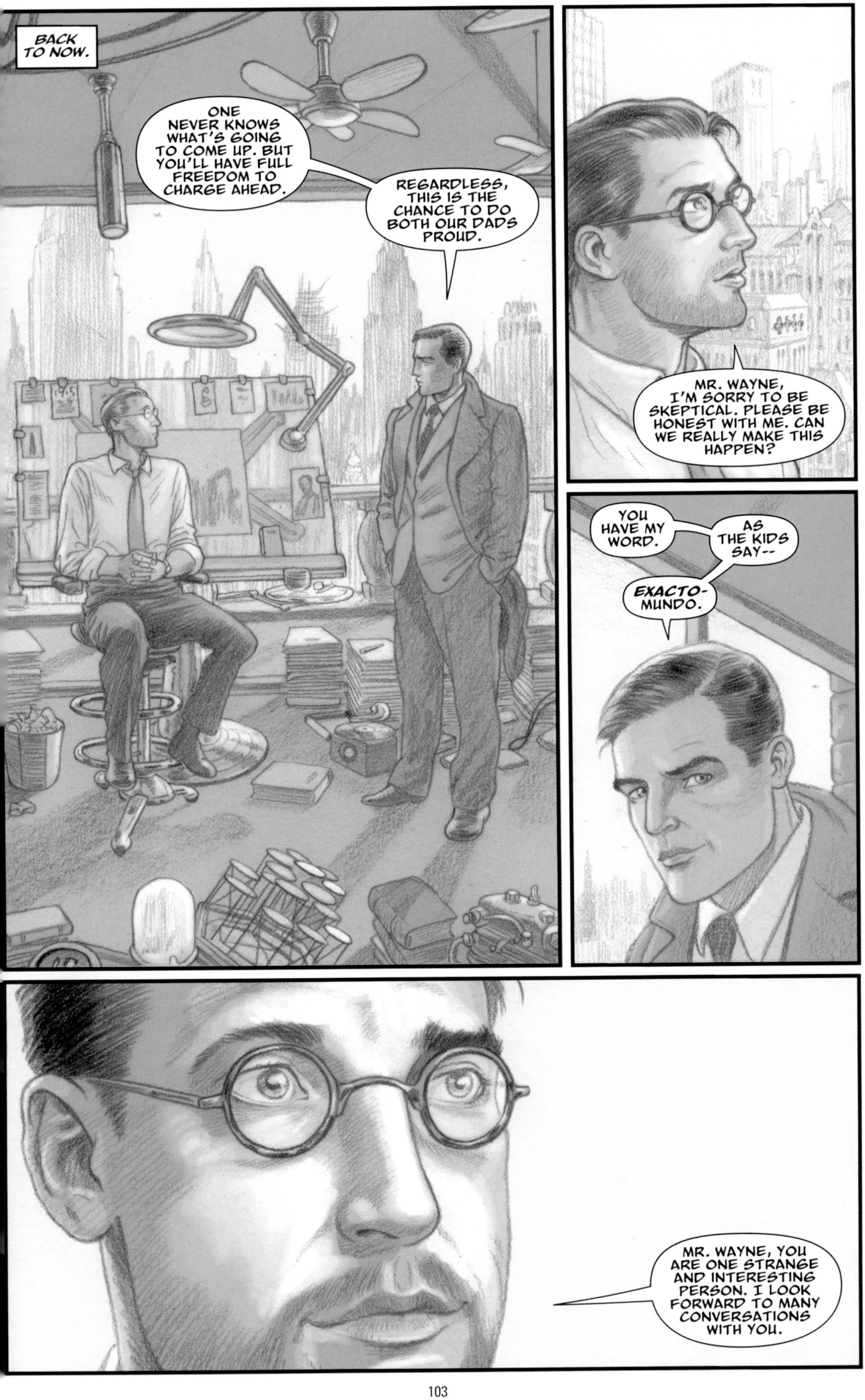

BACK TO NOW.
ONE NEVER KNOWS WHAT'S GOING TO COME UP. BUT YOU'LL HAVE FULL FREEDOM TO CHARGE AHEAD.
REGARDLESS, THIS IS THE CHANCE TO DO BOTH OUR DADS PROUD.

MR. WAYNE, I'M SORRY TO BE SKEPTICAL. PLEASE BE HONEST WITH ME. CAN WE REALLY MAKE THIS HAPPEN?

YOU HAVE MY WORD.
AS THE KIDS SAY--
EXACTO-MUNDO.

MR. WAYNE, YOU ARE ONE STRANGE AND INTERESTING PERSON. I LOOK FORWARD TO MANY CONVERSATIONS WITH YOU.

AS EVER.

GOTHAM WAYNE CENTRAL STATION

FINIS.

THANK YOU:

My friend, the architect Bart Voorsanger, spent a *lot* of time with me explaining the process and pitfalls of what it takes to actually design and build a skyscraper in Manhattan (look out for those ball-peen hammers!).

The endpapers were created in the spring of 2011 at a letterpress workshop I conducted at the Indiana University at Bloomington. I'm indebted to the incredibly gracious and skilled Paul Brown, who runs the program, and to Cristina Vanko and her fellow students who helped.

And thanks as always to Geoff Spear for shooting the drawings in the front and back, rendering their hand-made glory. —C. K.

A city-sized thank-you to Mark and Chip for their belief, support and patience!! —D. T.

Pages 2-3.

Double-page splash. Glorious, pan-o-ramic wide-screen view of Batman soaring up past the massive derelict station amidst the sky-line. In view nearby (in the background or off to the side--it should be there but not obtrusive) is a construction crane, nearly as tall as a skyscraper.

B, thought panel: "Will I miss it?"

CRANE

V DARK SKY
FG INC WCS
BLACK ON SKY
FADING OFF

BAT SEP

SKETCHBOOK.

COMMENTARY BY DAVE TAYLOR

"I've never had to study so hard as I did for DbD. The months of research and reference sourcing, experimenting and developing. I wanted everything in this book to feel real, authentic and true to the setting."

"It's a magical experience, quickly drawing out the story as I read, visualising a person's thoughts. It's Voodoo!"
Page 42, panel 1.
They are out of the elevator, which is separate from the cab itself, and entering the cab.
BL, speech balloon : "Let me show you something."
Page 42, panel 2.
Interior of the cab, which is small but impressive. There is room for about four people. Bart and Richard sit before the relatively large and complex operator's control panel. Through the windshield is the city below them, stretched out for miles in all directions. Loar is lighting a cigar.
BL, speech balloon : "I meant *real*, working, men, who bust their humps for an honest day's wage. Every day."
WINDOWS
Page 42, panel 3.
Loar, taking a puff, looking out over the cityscape.
BL, speech balloon: "Let me tell you something, kid."
BL, speech balloon, continued: "Four generations of my family built this city."
Page 42, panel 4.
Loar, slightly different angle, exhaling.
BL, speech balloon : "The first one did it for slave wages and an early grave."
BL, speech balloon, continued: "The second one fought to organize and survive."
Page 42, panel 5.
Loar, yet another angle, pointing the cigar at Richard (off panel).
BL, speech balloon : "The third figured out how to unite and thrive. "
BL, speech balloon , continued: "And the fourth one . . . rules."
Page 42, panel 6.
On Richard, trying to maintain his composure, pencil and pad in hand.
RF, speech balloon: "That's very . . . inspiring. So, can we start the interview?"
Page 42, panel 7.
On Loar's face, imperious.
BL, speech balloon: "Interview's over."
Page 42, panel 8.
On Richard's face, incredulous.
RF: "What?!!"
Page 42, panel 9.
Loar, now with as evil and menacing a leer as we've seen so far.
BL, speech balloon : "Now you listen to me. I am going back down. *You* will stay up here, and think long and hard about how you're going to proceed. Understand?"
RF, speech balloon, from off-panel: "I--"

"I doodle, not sketch. I learnt from Alex Toth to get it right on a small scale or it won't work. 98% of the time I'll end up using my first idea, the image that pops as I read a script is inevitably the one that'll get published."

THE
BATMAN

"All the work in this book is produced with good old- fashioned pencils, first in blue and then 'inked' in graphite. I made no corrections with an eraser; what I drew got published. The shading and color I overlaid on computer. This is my most 'honest' work!"

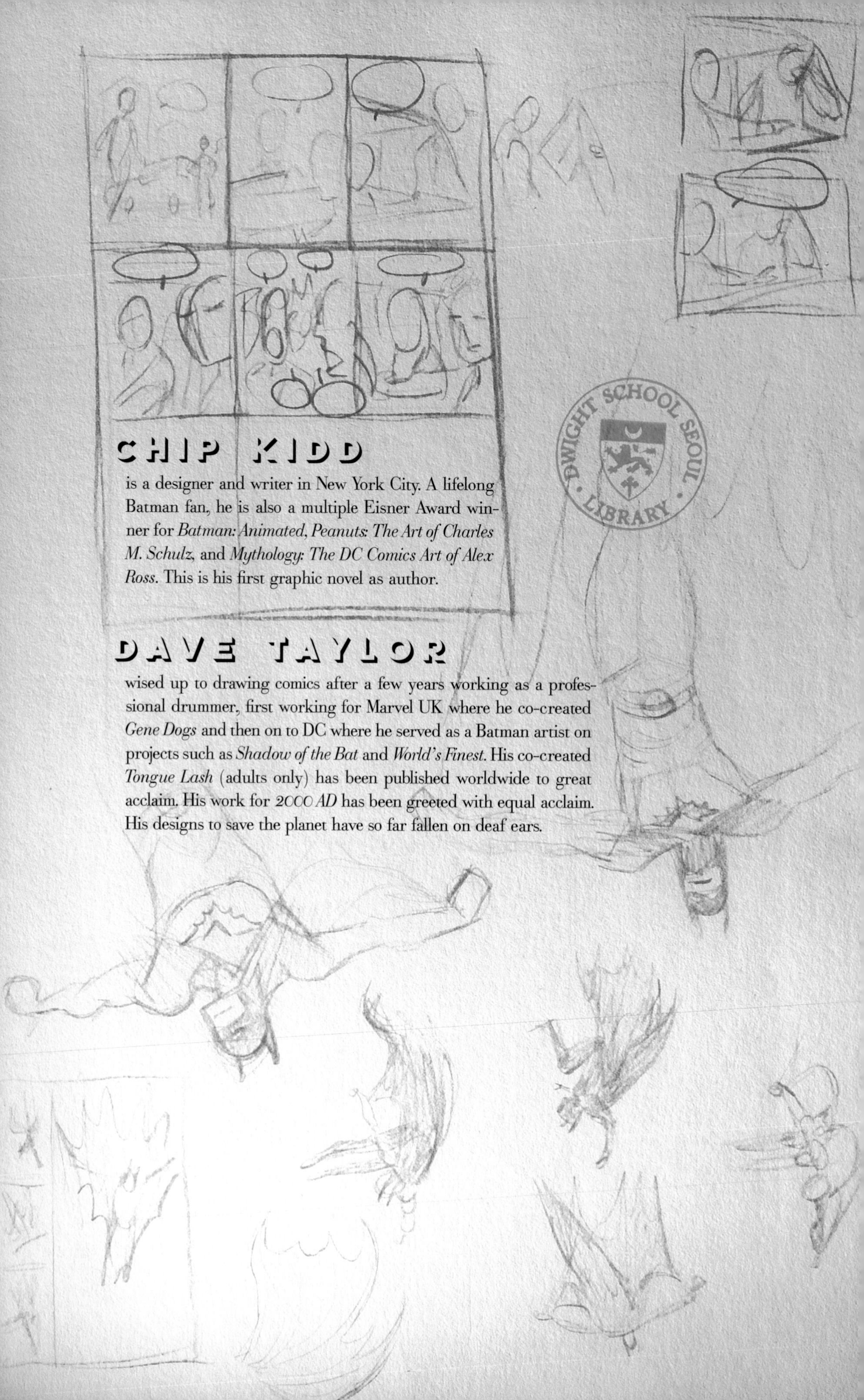

CHIP KIDD

is a designer and writer in New York City. A lifelong Batman fan, he is also a multiple Eisner Award winner for *Batman: Animated*, *Peanuts: The Art of Charles M. Schulz*, and *Mythology: The DC Comics Art of Alex Ross*. This is his first graphic novel as author.

DAVE TAYLOR

wised up to drawing comics after a few years working as a professional drummer, first working for Marvel UK where he co-created *Gene Dogs* and then on to DC where he served as a Batman artist on projects such as *Shadow of the Bat* and *World's Finest*. His co-created *Tongue Lash* (adults only) has been published worldwide to great acclaim. His work for *2000 AD* has been greeted with equal acclaim. His designs to save the planet have so far fallen on deaf ears.

DEA

DES

A Thrilli

Pictur

only from

DC

AVAILABLE AT YOU